UNDERSTANDING JOHN EDGAR WIDEMAN

UNDERSTANDING CONTEMPORARY AMERICAN LITERATURE

Matthew J. Bruccoli, Founding Editor

Linda Wagner-Martin, Series Editor

UNDERSTANDING JOHN EDGAR WIDEMAN

D. Quentin Miller

The University of South Carolina Press

Published by the University of South Carolina Press
Columbia, South Carolina 29208

www.sc.edu/uscpress

Manufactured in the United States of America

27 26 25 24 23 22 21 20 19 18 10 9 8 7 6 5 4 3 2 1

Library of Congress Cataloging-in-Publication Data
can be found at http://catalog.loc.gov/.

ISBN: 978-1-61117-824-1 (hardcover)
ISBN: 978-1-61117-825-8 (ebook)

This book was printed on recycled paper with
30 percent postconsumer waste content.

To Julie

CONTENTS

SERIES EDITOR'S PREFACE

The Understanding Contemporary American Literature series was founded by the estimable Matthew J. Bruccoli (1931–2008), who envisioned these volumes as guides or companions for students as well as good nonacademic readers, a legacy that will continue as new volumes are developed to fill in gaps among the nearly one hundred series volumes published to date and to embrace a host of new writers only now making their marks on our literature.

As Professor Bruccoli explained in his preface to the volumes he edited, because much influential contemporary literature makes special demands, "the word understanding in the titles was chosen deliberately. Many willing readers lack an adequate understanding of how contemporary literature works; that is, of what the author is attempting to express and the means by which it is conveyed." Aimed at fostering this understanding of good literature and good writers, the criticism and analysis in the series provide instruction in how to read certain contemporary writers—explicating their material, language, structures, themes, and perspectives—and facilitate a more profitable experience of the works under discussion.

In the twenty-first century Professor Bruccoli's prescience gives us an avenue to publish expert critiques of significant contemporary American writing. The series continues to map the literary landscape and to provide both instruction and enjoyment. Future volumes will seek to introduce new voices alongside canonized favorites, to chronicle the changing literature of our times, and to remain, as Professor Bruccoli conceived, contemporary in the best sense of the word.

Linda Wagner-Martin, Series Editor

ACKNOWLEDGMENTS

I would like to thank a group of students in my Selected African American Writers course (fall 2013) who resisted *Hoop Roots* so much that it made me look at Wideman more deeply than I ever had before. Thanks also to Suffolk University for granting me a sabbatical leave to get my work done and to the Boston Athenaeum for giving me a spectacular space in which to complete it.

CHAPTER 1

Understanding John Edgar Wideman

The point isn't replicating some other writer. The point is expressing myself, being myself.

Wideman, *God's Gym,* 173

I demand that readers meet me halfway, that they participate and think and open themselves up to confronting some stuff that maybe they haven't thought about before, some feelings they're not willing to own up to. To that extent the very nature of what I do means if I'm not upsetting somebody, not getting under their skin in some way, what I'm doing is probably not working.

TuSmith, *Conversations with John Edgar Wideman,* 144

These two epigraphs capture something of the defiance, confidence, and challenges of John Edgar Wideman's work. Wideman is a tough writer in every sense of the word: a man who has been hardened by the circumstances of his life, who writes about difficult subjects in a difficult style, and who is not afraid to examine wounds or even to dig deeper into wounds to analyze their causes and effects. His works resist categorization, and he does not fit neatly with the other African American writers who flourished in the post–Black Arts Movement era of the 1970s and 1980s. Toni Morrison might provide the closest comparison: both authors are concerned with black history (and both have a particular fascination with the murder of Emmett Till), both write about family, both are comfortable moving between esoteric allusions and black vernacular speech ("the academy and the street,"[1] in Wideman's words), and both confront trauma and damage as they produce works that cannot be fully understood or appreciated in a single reading. And yet the comparison does not hold up for long. Morrison tends to focus on female characters, while Wideman's universe is predominately masculine. Morrison's works are rarely autobiographical, whereas Wideman's often are. As Keith Byerman has argued, "Unlike Morrison, Wideman offers little optimism," at least in the first half of his career.[2] Finally, Morrison's works have been widely read and lauded, culminating in her winning the Nobel Prize for Literature in 1993. Although Wideman has been recognized with a MacArthur Grant and a handful of prominent literary prizes, literary history has not been as kind to him, and he has certainly not enjoyed the widespread readership that Morrison has.

Regarded as a quirky genius following the publication of his first three novels in the late 1960s and early 1970s, Wideman deliberately retrenched and reemerged in the 1980s to great acclaim with three works of fiction together known as the Homewood Trilogy (1981–83), his memoir *Brothers and Keepers* (1984), and a flurry of other books. This blistering output of impressive work continued into the 1990s. Since then, his writing has slowed considerably, and his works published in the last decade have not enjoyed anything like the attention his earlier ones received, particularly those from the 1980s. True to the statements that serve as the epigraphs above, though, he has never been a writer who sought mainstream fame or who pandered to readers who were not willing to do the hard work of engaging with the layers of his work. His oeuvre represents the relentless struggle to understand and communicate a difficult, complex vision. Readers who approach him casually are likely to be confused. Readers who dedicate themselves to his work are likely to be rewarded (if also exhausted) intellectually, aesthetically, and emotionally.

Life and Career

Wideman was born on June 14, 1941, in Washington, D.C. His mother, Bette French, and his father, Edgar Wideman, figure prominently in his fiction and nonfiction. It could even be argued that a primary tension in Wideman's work is an attempt to resolve the aspects of his parents' personalities that trace back through their lineage: his mother's unstinting religious faith and perseverance versus his father's distant stoicism. His first name is an homage to his grandfather John French, a nearly mythical figure in his work, who exuded life and energy until his ignoble death in a bathroom. In Wideman's story "Backseat," meditating on the nature of names, he writes, "When I published my first novel, I wanted my father's name to be part of the record so I was John Edgar Wideman on the cover. Now the three names of my entitles sound pretentious to me, stiff and old-fashioned. I'd prefer to be just plain John Wideman, but can't shake the Edgar" (*All Stories* 42). Metaphorically, Wideman cannot shake his family, or his fate, or his connection to his father, who is rendered as a distant figure, a bully, and an isolated old man at various places in his work.

Wideman was the oldest of five siblings raised in the Homewood and Shadyside neighborhoods of Pittsburgh. Shadyside was a white-dominated neighborhood, and although moving there afforded him certain opportunities through access to better schools, the family had to move back to Homewood because of financial struggles. Homewood was in a period of decline, and like his neighborhood, Wideman's family deteriorated over time. In a late story about his mother, "Weight," he describes how she persevered "in spite of a son in prison for life, twin girls born dead, a mind-blown son who roams the streets with everything he owns in a shopping cart, a strung-out daughter with a crack baby, a good daughter who miscarried the only child her dry womb ever produced, in spite of me and the rest of my limp-along, near-to-normal siblings and their children—my nephews doping and gangbanging, nieces unwed, underage, dropping babies as regularly as the seasons" (*God's Gym* 2). The dire circumstances of his family unfolded gradually over the course of his life. Wideman's upbringing did not forecast the remarkable (and perhaps exaggerated) family dysfunction detailed here. His Homewood years were not rosy, but they did not resemble this kind of devastation. Many of his renditions of his early family life describe a matriarchy in which his mother, grandmother, and aunts largely raised him while his father worked a series of jobs to support the family. Wideman had to take his masculine cues from his peers, particularly on urban basketball courts, which became a recurrent setting his work, especially in the latter half of his oeuvre.

Recognized for his intellect from an early age, Wideman was awarded a scholarship to the University of Pennsylvania, where he played basketball and studied the largely white literary canon, particularly the European modernists such as James Joyce and T. S. Eliot, who influenced his early novels. His years at an Ivy League school were intellectually stimulating and foundational, but they also intensified feelings of racial alienation that deeply scarred him. In *Brothers and Keepers* he recalls one particular incident when a "smartass, whole-lot-hipper-than-you"[3] white student challenged his taste in music, claiming, of all things, that he did not understand the blues. This challenge provoked in Wideman a complex mix of anger and self-consciousness about his status as a black man trying to succeed in a largely white world. He sometimes came to view his college experience as flight rather than journey, or as a ticket out of Homewood rather than the keys to a kingdom. His higher education continued with a Rhodes Scholarship to Oxford, where he wrote his thesis on an eighteenth-century precursor of the postmodern novel, Laurence Sterne's *Tristram Shandy*. He returned to the University of Pennsylvania as the first tenured black professor of English. A watershed moment occurred when a group of black students approached him in 1968 and asked him to teach a course in black literature. He turned them down, claiming he did not know enough about that literary tradition to teach it. This conversation brought him up short and caused him to retreat for nearly a decade while he read black literature intensely and turned for source material to the neighborhood in Pittsburgh where he grew up—Homewood—to listen to family stories and retell them as closely as possible to the way they were communicated to him. Although his later works do not replicate the techniques he used in the Homewood Trilogy, this period left an indelible mark on his work, not only in its emphasis on authentic voices but also on the attention he pays to the workings of stories.

In 1973, following his time as a professor at Penn, Wideman traveled with his wife, Judy, and their two sons to Laramie, Wyoming, where he accepted a position at the university there. It was during this period that he returned to Homewood in his imagination, but Homewood also came to him, quite literally, in a way that would forever change the trajectory of his work. On November 15, 1975, his brother Robby was involved in a botched robbery in Pittsburgh that resulted in a senseless murder. Robby and his coconspirators went on the lam and ended up at John's house in Wyoming. They were caught and arrested soon afterward, and Robby was sentenced to life in prison. Wideman's attempts to connect with his incarcerated brother and to argue for his release provided the raw material for a good deal of his fiction and nonfiction.

In the mid-1980s Wideman returned to the East Coast, specifically to the University of Massachusetts, where he taught from 1986 to 2004. It was during this time that another murder altered the trajectory of his career. In 1986 his son Jacob, then sixteen, suffered what might be considered a psychotic break and acted on a dark fantasy he had been harboring throughout his troubled youth: during a summer camp in Arizona, he murdered his roommate and was arrested after a weak attempt at flight. Wideman's willingness to go deep into his brother's experience in prison is balanced by his reluctance to explore his son's. The incident and all that surrounds it is clearly too painful for Wideman to write about except in limited or indirect ways. Tellingly, in a 1997 interview in response to a question about how he exposes his personal life in his work, he said, "I'm spilling precisely the amount that I want to spill. It's always revealing and concealing. If I show you my bleeding hand, it may be because I don't want you to see my bleeding foot."[4] The relationship between fathers and sons is another recurrent touchstone in his work, and the traumatic disruption of his own efforts to be a good father has intensified this motif considerably.

It is clear that this event also put a irremediable strain on his marriage. In 2000 Wideman and his wife, Judy, divorced after thirty-five years of marriage.

In addition to Jacob, the couple raised two other children—Daniel, a writer and editor at Lulu Books, a small press that published Wideman's most recent story collection (*Briefs,* 2010), and Jamila, who was featured on the cover of *Sports Illustrated* (March 17, 1997) as a standout basketball player at Stanford (she went on to star in the WNBA). His late writings, notably *The Island: Martinique,* discuss his relationship with Catherine Nedonchelle, a French writer whom he married in 2004. Since retiring from Brown University in 2014, Wideman has largely retreated from the public eye.

In contrast with his prolific output in the 1980s and 1990s, Wideman has produced very little in recent years. After a six-year hiatus he recently published *Writing to Save A Life* (2016) about the father of Emmett Till. His most recent novel, *Fanon* (2008), reveals his weariness with his writing career in no uncertain terms, and his most recent story collection, *Briefs* (2010), is a collection of flash fiction, a stripped-down form that marks a clear departure from the long-form memoirs and novels from his most successful period. In his recent work he reveals his frustration with the way his culture has devolved, with the way his family has disintegrated, and with the reception of serious literary authors in a world increasingly given over to the sound bites of superficial media.

It is possible that Wideman has other tricks up his sleeve in the twilight of his career. He is known, after all, for publishing his best-known works (the Homewood Trilogy and *Brothers and Keepers*) after a seven-year disappearing act. Still, his recent works have revealed a weariness that would not have been imaginable when he was at the apex of his career, publishing prolifically, winning awards, and teaching. He was ubiquitous in the early 1990s, writing in a prominent magazine about the Rodney King riots, receiving his second PEN/Faulkner award in 1993 as well as a MacArthur "Genius Grant," editing the *Best American Short Stories* in 1996, and publishing groundbreaking meditations on the intersection of race and incarceration. The moment is perhaps right for Wideman to be reassessed and rediscovered, given the complexity of our current period of racial unrest. He will be most useful not as a goldmine of slogans or proclamations but as an earnest artist who stared hard at a long history of personal and collective suffering and did not flinch.

Reception

Tracie Church Guzzio, one of the prominent critics of Wideman's work, has pointed to "a paucity of scholarship on Wideman"[5] in her 2011 study. Indeed, the critical monographs on Wideman's contemporary Toni Morrison number in the hundreds, while there are currently fewer than ten critical books on Wideman, as well as a couple dozen important articles and a 1998 collection of interviews. The Wideman author society has endeavored to keep scholarship on Wideman alive at the annual American Literature Association convention, but attendance at their panels has dwindled in recent years. Wideman's diminished output and public withdrawal has probably contributed to the problem, coupled with the fact that one of his most recent books *(Briefs)* was put out by a small publisher, having considerably little commercial potential. This fate would have been difficult to predict in the 1980s and 1990s when Wideman was producing a steady flow of critically acclaimed work. There was an entire conference dedicated to his writings at the University of Virginia in 2000. The rich, dense nature of his writing, the intensity of his subject matter, and the force of his intellect position him for a strong revival in upcoming years, much as his literary forefather James Baldwin—who had faded into obscurity in the years before his death in 1987 despite having been the most prominent black author of the early 1960s—has enjoyed a spectacular critical revival in the twenty-first century.

Baldwin's and Wideman's careers are parallel in a number of ways. Intellectuals known for leaving the shabby neighborhoods of their youth for periods of expatriation (notably in Europe), both have suffered because they occasionally countered assumptions about what black writers should write about. Baldwin's second novel, *Giovanni's Room* (1956), about white bisexual characters trying to come to terms with their identity in Paris, raised more than a few eyebrows, especially after his first two books had spoken about race in more expected ways. Wideman's first two novels focus nearly as much on the dilemmas of aging, alcoholic white men as they focus on the alienated young black men who encounter them. Both authors exhibit artistic and intellectual skills that could be described as intimidating. Both were occasionally accused of being out of touch with the world they wrote about because of their tendency to spend time in exile. And in interviews and their writings, both have come across as being indifferent to the opinions of their detractors or their dwindling readership, following the empowering message of Langston Hughes in his famous 1926 essay "The Negro Artist and the Racial Mountain," which concludes with the conviction that black artists have to be true to their own vision rather than to try to please audiences, whether they are black or white.

The imprisoned journalist Mumia Abu-Jamal wrote of Wideman as a representative of his generation for whom the integration of white and black America "became a virtual recipe for estrangement."[6] James Coleman, in the first book-length study on Wideman, spoke of a "progression" from "his depiction of the black intellectual's isolation from the black community" to "the black intellectual in a meaningful relationship with the black community."[7] Although it might have been easy to affirm this assessment in the late 1980s when Coleman's study was published, largely as an endorsement of the Homewood

Trilogy, it would be much harder to accept it now. Wideman's work does not conform easily to a simple formula like "progression," and if anything, his recent works such as *Fanon* reveal an artist whose feelings of alienation are at least as strong as they had been in his early works. The interviews collected in Bonnie TuSmith's 1998 collection present some tension around assumptions about what black writers should or must write about. Wideman comes across as wary of such questions and reluctant to get trapped into the rhetoric of race, a concept he evaluates in a sophisticated way in *Fatheralong* and elsewhere.

Coleman's work provided a stepping stone for some critics who followed (notably Dorothea Mbalia in her 1995 study) and a roadblock for others. Coleman's tendency to divide Wideman's works into those that fail or succeed according to the way they embrace or eschew the notion of black community provides one legitimate inroad into the complexity of the arc of Wideman's career but also tends to constrain readings of Wideman's work that are more nuanced. The works associated with Homewood are outnumbered by the rest of Wideman's oeuvre, but the Homewood books are often held up as the pinnacle of his achievement while the others are devalued. Recent critics have had to work hard to move past the assumptions of Coleman's study in order to develop new interpretations of Wideman's work and/or to delve deeper into it. This trend does not hold in Europe, however, where criticism of Wideman's work (showcased in a special issue of *Callaloo* in 1999) is far ranging. Book-length studies by Keith Byerman and Guzzio and a collection edited by Byerman and TuSmith[8] in recent years have built on a host of articles on Wideman to demonstrate that the fullness and richness of his work are now being explored more thoroughly in academic circles even as his popular readership has declined.

Themes and Features of Wideman's Writing

Wideman is known primarily for his meditations on race, which, like most of his other frequent subjects, are as conscious of culture and history as they are reflective of individual experience. In a 1995 interview he summarized the association between his writing and questions of black identity: "writing, any art, has something to do with the culture, and given certain formations of African American culture, yes, key issues—oppression, poverty, violence, for instance—are foregrounded whether you like it or not. But there is always more to a group than its sociological profile."[9] He frequently underscores the distinction between art and sociology and is wary of the kind of thinking that reduces a subtle, complex exploration of the meaning of "race." There are many instances in his work when characters who think purely in terms of race find themselves in dangerous situations: in the novel *The Lynchers* (1973) a group of black men conspire to hang a white policeman as a symbolic gesture, but the plan also involves the murder of a black prostitute and results in the death of one of the group's members. In *Sent for You Yesterday* (1983) a black woman attempts to strengthen her race by having a multitude of black children and protecting them in her house, which she calls "the ark"; but when she gives birth to a light-skinned boy, the other children participate in his destruction. In a lengthy meditation on the dreaded "paradigm of race" in *Fatheralong* (1998), he expresses his more measured take on race cogently: "I don't need to hate white people in order to love myself. But I also don't need white people to tell me what I am or what I can strive to be or tell me if I've made it or not" (xxiv). The horrors of the past stemming from (but not limited to) slavery weigh heavily on him; and yet he has also managed to navigate the predominately white world at Penn, Oxford, the University of Wyoming, the University of Massachusetts, and Brown University, not to mention the white publishing world or (on a personal level) long-term relationships with white women. Perhaps this is why Ishmael Reed has dubbed Wideman "a mulatto writer, neither black nor white."[10] Wideman might be the first to question why the same term might not be defined as "both black and white," but then again, alienation is perhaps his most prominent subject.

If there is a consistent feature of Wideman's writing, it involves confrontation in an attempt to reconcile various opposing forces. In his introduction to *The Best American Stories of 1996,* he wrote, "Given our country's history, our history before it was a country, you'd think the most American theme would be the inevitability of difference, the pain and consolation difference confers."[11] Race is the explicit context for this observation, but one might point to class or gender as other fields where difference provides both pain and consolation. Wideman has examined both male and female worlds, though perhaps not with the same success with which he has managed to navigate race or class. He insisted in one interview that "the models of eloquence that were most important . . . were the women in my family," but in another interview he bristled when a female interviewer labeled one of his characters a misogynist and claimed that this character's thinking is "unrelenting in its degradation of the female."[12] His upbringing as described in memoirs such as *Fatheralong* and *Hoop Roots* (2001) reveals that he was largely raised by his mother, grandmother, and aunts, but that he was constantly in search of male heroes, role models, and companions. His most thoroughly developed fictional characters tend to be men, and it is fair to say that women do not often hold positions of authority or power in his work. Detractors might suggest that they are too frequently rendered as the objects of male sexual desire (with notable exceptions). There is a good deal of sexual content throughout his work, but it is often depicted in terms of contention rather than pleasure. In one memorable exchange in *Hoop Roots,* he browbeats a lover to share sex stories from her past. He recognizes his suspicious motives in coercing her do this, and although she complies, she quickly retreats into a damaged, private space. Some of Wideman's descriptions of sex border on the uncomfortable because of their frank nature and intensity, but as he reveals in the second epigraph above, he believes that he has done his job if his readers feel upset in some way.

Stylistically, Wideman is in his own category. Critics regarded his first two novels as an outgrowth of literary modernism, largely because they allude heavily to James Joyce and T. S. Eliot, and because their narrative methods, such as stream-of-consciousness, resemble those of novelists such as William Faulkner. During the high years of his career, critics were more likely to label Wideman a postmodernist, especially given his tendency to interrupt his stories to reveal the author's perspective and to demonstrate his consciousness of the ways in which stories work. But neither of these labels sticks for very long. Wideman is a writer who rarely writes the same way twice, even though he treats the same subjects repeatedly and even tells the same stories in different contexts. His work is saturated with the authentic speech of the people he knew on the streets of Homewood, or on the basketball court, or in his family. At the same time, he can construct sentences of dizzying lengths using erudite vocabulary and obscure allusions. Byerman has argued that Wideman's willingness to combine black vernacular traditions with postmodern techniques is a strength rather than a contradiction: "he locates in them a connection, in, first, a digressive style that permits the introduction of different discourses, and second, the recovery of voices that are often suppressed."[13] Susan Pearsall quipped that his works are "more or less inaccessible to readers lacking at least a college education,"[14] and TuSmith suggested that he "challenges his readers at every level."[15] He occasionally indulges in linguistic tours de force in which he puns and plays on the multiple meanings of words. As his brother Robby says to him in *Fanon,* "Funny, you know, the craziest shit's what I like best. When you get off on words and get to rapping and signifying and shit" (64). The fact that this line is delivered in Robby's voice testifies to Wideman's range and complexity.

Fueling his unique, ever-changing style is a willingness to experiment. In a 1983 interview he said, "Any writing is a form of adventure, a form of play, a form of fun. Very serious play, and very difficult and involving play. The idea of writing a fairly conventional narrative, a plot that requires a fairly straightforward development, a novel that could be used as a model in bogus creative writing courses—that has no interest for me."[16] Although it is possible to see recurrent patterns in Wideman's work and to classify them, each of his works is unique and a departure from all the others. Even the three books that constitute the Homewood Trilogy are very different from one another in terms of style, form, theme, and voice. Within Wideman's term "very serious play," many readers focus on the seriousness of his work, but the playfulness is important as well. The reader may get lost in a sentence that runs on for seventeen pages, but the author is clearly enjoying the freedom it gives him.

As a parallel to his writing, visual art is one of Wideman's recurrent obsessions. An early novel, *Hurry Home* (1970), is heavily steeped in descriptions of a painting by Hieronymus Bosch. Wideman is particularly interested in the sculptures of Alberto Giacometti and in the Italian sculptor's pronouncements about art. In the novel *Philadelphia Fire* (1990) he writes, "Alberto Giacometti revolted from his father Giovanni's aesthetic convention that known reality is identical with perceived reality" (146). Perception is a key concept in Wideman: the title of his first novel *A Glance Away* (1967) comes from Giacometti's belief that the world changes irrevocably whenever one's concentration shifts. In *God's Gym* (2008) he writes, "[Giacometti] understood art always failed. Art lied to him. People's eyes lied. No one ever sees the world as it is" (108). In the novel *Two Cities* (1998), he addresses Giacometti directly: "Invisible views. They are what attract me to your art. You force me to see something not there . . . our eyes take snapshots . . . from these snapshots we build a world of things with weight, shape, things that move and last. We believe in them. Depend on them" (91). He is also interested in the work of Eadweard Muybridge, the pioneering photographer who attempted to capture objects in motion. Language is for Wideman an attempt to freeze moments that the artist perceives, generally through memory. Storytelling is the motif that allows him to circle back to significant moments, not necessarily to ascertain the facts of what actually happened, but to demonstrate a broader truth about the way a mind perceives experience.

The subjects of Wideman's work are as diverse as his stylistic experiments, but there are a number of motifs that recur: family dynamics, incarceration, basketball, the way history affects black American psychology, the cities of Philadelphia and Pittsburgh, and the vital importance of stories. As Byerman notes, "He has taken virtually every aspect of his experience and made it material for his art. What makes his story worth telling is that he has found the dramatic and storytelling possibilities in the things that most of us either merely accept, or dismiss, or try to conceal."[17] The attentive reader of Wideman's work is likely to finish a book with more questions than answers—sophisticated questions that will leave him or her thinking. As he says in *Hoop Roots,* "A story expresses the unique name of something, doesn't try to explain something" (194).

Wideman's literary influences, in addition to the aforementioned white modernists, are also varied, although he has declined to name them as such, saying that "citing individuals as heroes or whatnot is like foregrounding an all-star team instead of foregrounding the game."[18] He dedicated one book to W. E. B. DuBois, whose famous theory of double-consciousness permeates Wideman's work. In a textbook example of DuBois's theory, he told an interviewer,

> You can say that "Wideman is a good writer; he uses Afro-American folklore, he knows this, that, or the other thing about his heritage and culture." You can make that argument, and show it in the work, and pat me on the back, but that doesn't get me out of the ghetto. It should, but it doesn't. If I do all that, I mean that is enough, but there is always an implied, invidious comparison: "OK, Wideman does fine with Afro-American stuff, but on the other hand the real writers are doing so and so. . . ." To protect ourselves as critics and artists, we are forced to jump back and forth, measure ourselves against an imaginary mainstream, define what we are doing in somebody else's terms. It's almost like making excuses. It is a terrible bind.[19]

In addition to DuBois, there are also frequent allusions in Wideman's work to Ellison's *Invisible Man* and occasionally to James Baldwin, whom he met in Amherst when they both taught there in the late 1980s and about whom he claimed to "owe a tremendous debt to the example of his work implicitly and explicitly."[20] In a story in *God's Gym* he writes the following about the Black Arts Movement standard-bearer Amiri Baraka: "*The world is full of remarkable things* . . . One of my favorite lines from one of my favorite writers. Back in the day when I still pretended books worth talking about, people were surprised to discover Baraka a favorite of mine, as quietly integrated and nonconfrontational a specimen as I seemed to be of America's longest, most violently reviled minority" (104). It is not so much Baraka's politics or style that he admires but "the chances he'd taken, chances in his art, in his life" (104).

Art and politics have a vexed relationship in Wideman's work. In an interview with Ishmael Reed, he described how "annoyed" he becomes "when people talk about rage in my fiction. . . . I'm the Prince of Rage. It sells books, I guess, or it makes reviews."[21] If there is one particular topic that consistently stirs him to action, if not to rage, it is the prison system. His analysis of the state of incarceration in America and his frequent calls for reform certainly put him at the vanguard of conversations about the confluence of prisons and the black community. In a 1999 essay in the *Nation*, he observed, "Prison itself, with its unacceptably large percentage of men and women of color, is being transformed by the street values and street needs of a younger generation of prisoners to mirror the conditions of urban war zones and accommodate a fluid population who know their lives will involve inevitable shuttling between prison and the street."[22] In his introduction to Abu-Jamal's *Live from Death Row* (1995), he wrote, "Prison walls are being proposed as a final solution. They symbolize our shortsightedness, our fear of the real problems caging us all. The pity is how blindly, enthusiastically, we applaud those who are constructing the walls dooming us" (xxix). *Brothers and Keepers,* perhaps his best-known work, is a groundbreaking book in terms of the way it bears witness to the prison experience, especially insofar as prisons affect the families of the incarcerated.

Even though some of his more recent essays indicate an increased willingness to weigh in on current political issues, Wideman is an author primarily concerned with the self, particularly with the individual mind. Instances of social rebellion in his work—such as a plot to kill a white police officer in *The Lynchers* or his brother Robby's attempts at social activism in his high school, as described in numerous places—do not seem to produce lasting social change. His most recent novel is purportedly about the revolutionary Frantz Fanon, but it is actually about the way his own overactive creative mind prevents him from telling Fanon's story in a straightforward way so that people such as his brother, who are not particularly bookish, might understand it. His brother says, "I give you credit for being an intelligent guy, but, you know, I got to wonder if writing an intelligent book's an intelligent idea" (164). For all of Baraka's abstraction, he was trying to reach a mass audience. Wideman did so in the Homewood books in which he was deliberately publishing books "accessible to a wide Black audience"[23] (as he himself described it), but despite this accessibility, it is still difficult to say where he stands on a number of issues that might be deemed "political." Byerman has classified him "as one of a group of writers—including Toni Morrison, Ernest Gaines, and Charles Johnson—who immersed their readers in black history and culture without being committed to a particular political or social agenda."[24] The complexity of Wideman's thought process and his interpretation of the nature of art make it impossible to locate a straightforward political statement in his writing. Racism is an enduring subject within his work, but one cannot boil down his thick meditations on that subject into a coherent "message." There are certainly recurrent motifs, though, that form a pattern: Wideman resists ideology and prefabricated notions of the truth; he is suspicious of systems that rob individuals of intellectual autonomy; he holds individuals and families above institutions; and he is deeply interested in expressions of folk culture, not as inherently pure or wise but as legitimate records of experience that should be taken seriously.

Two of these expressions of folk culture are recurrent subjects in his work: basketball and blues music. Both were compromised by his experiences in the Ivy League. He said in a 1985 interview, "I learned to play kind of freelance, spontaneous, improvisational basketball. But for college basketball you had to learn systems, you had to put yourself within this kind of disciplined, coach-centered style. What I did was playground basketball and they erased that from the kids who came in."[25] His 2001 book *Hoop Roots* is an attempt to redraw what had been erased, to get readers to appreciate the deep meaning of playground hoop as a nearly sacred ritual and an art form, "like classic African-American jazz" (48). Wideman consistently compares his own method of writing to jazz as well, particularly in terms of hard work and improvisation. Blues—a variation on jazz—is a recurrent motif in his work. We hear strains of it within the prose, as when Tommy in *Hiding Place* (1981) is heard humming the blues or when his aunt Bess in that same work tells the story of her man singing his personal version of the blues. Brother, a main character in *Sent for You Yesterday*, substitutes scatting for actual speech. Moreover, as Guzzio has argued, "The blues hero is a consistent character, repeated and revised throughout Wideman's work."[26] Although the blues hero has many characteristics, chief among them is the ability to convert suffering into survival. To some degree Wideman himself can be defined this way, and although it would be reductive to say that his works resemble the blues, it might be accurate to say that they are all variations on the blues as heard and retold by John Edgar Wideman.

CHAPTER 2

The First Three Novels

Critics tend to separate Wideman's first three novels—*A Glance Away* (1967), *Hurry Home* (1970), and *The Lynchers* (1973)—from the rest of his work, and to deem them inferior. The general critique is that they are too imitative of white modernist classics and thus removed from Wideman's own experience and the voices of the people he once knew in Homewood. In a 1985 interview with Kay Bonetti, he underwrote this opinion to some degree. "What do you value about the first three books?" she asked. He responded, "I don't look back that often. The work that's past is gone."[1] Although he did admit that his early works were valuable for a number of reasons—"experiments with language, experiments with form, bringing to the fore black cultural material, history, archetypes, myths, the language itself"—he also said, "I think I had my priorities a little bit mixed up. I felt that I had to prove something about black speech, for instance, and about black culture, and that they needed to be imbedded within the larger literary frame."[2] The break between these first three works and the rest of his oeuvre is clear but perhaps not as dramatic as some critics have believed, and Guzzio has argued persuasively that these works are foundational.[3] The Homewood Trilogy (chapter 3) and subsequent works appear less burdened by the weight of literary history than the first three novels are, or at least less "connected to Europe,"[4] as Wideman said in the same interview; but the balancing act between university-learned erudition and folk wisdom evident in the early work is a constant in Wideman's work.

A Glance Away is an ambitious first novel that initiates one of Wideman's prominent motifs: the exile and tortured return of an alienated young man. Although there is a large cast of characters, the intergenerational and interracial novel centers around Eddie Lawson, the only surviving male child in a black family. He is friends with a tragic figure named Brother Small, also black but with white skin through albinism, and Brother's story is entangled with that of Robert Thurley, a white, alcoholic English professor who conducts illicit affairs with young black men. There is a clear battle between Eddie and Thurley, but it is only about race on the surface. The deeper story examines the way men with overactive minds cope with their troubled pasts.

The novel's prologue is a lyrical montage of scenes of birth, sex, and death. The language is inventive, alliterative, mythical, and strongly reminiscent of great modernist novels by James Joyce or William Faulkner. Joycean neologisms like "afterall" and "dedecorumed" are interspersed with passages in which the charming family patriarch, DaddyGene, sings folk tunes and speaks in a black vernacular, high on wine, as he visits his daughter, who has just given birth to his grandson. DaddyGene—the earliest representation of Wideman's grandfather John French—is larger than life, a family god who shows equal enthusiasm for his work (hanging wallpaper) and his family life, although his tendency to overindulge in wine compromises both. The novel opens with the birth of his namesake, couched in nearly biblical terms: "And he shall be called Eugene" (3). The birth of his second grandson, Eddie, is much less ceremonial and tinged with tragedy: "From a height, from a blessed height another fell, wingless, full of grief, sorrowing even as he plunged down through the darkness. Splat" (12). Eddie's pessimism begins with this indelicate birth. His father is absent, his mother is young and scared, and his grandmother is ineffective and disapproving. His grandfather alone offers the spirit of life.

The "splat" of Eddie's birth is connected to the central action of the prologue: DaddyGene carries the young boy to church on his shoulders so that they can watch the spiritual exuberance of the church members. All the while he spits tobacco, which lands with a "splat" each time. The "splat" echoes again at DaddyGene's funeral as a clod of shoveled earth lands on his coffin. The prologue highlights the cycle of birth, sex, and death. Echoes of T. S. Eliot's poem *The Waste Land* in the prologue make the theme of compromised fertility prominent. The tobacco juice DaddyGene spits is a foul rain that lands on a landscape riddled with death, and yet DaddyGene exudes life and fecundity. He celebrates his grandsons and imparts advice to Eddie while they picnic on a verdant lawn. Faced with the burdens of a hero, Eddie has to find his way in the world without any male elders to guide him. His confusion as an adult stems from his inability to reconcile his role with his personality, tinged from birth with grief and sorrow. This character type—a man destined for greatness but incapable of personal happiness—is common throughout Wideman's work and can be read as a representation of the author.

The novel proper opens with Eddie's return from an asylum on Easter

Sunday. He and his brother, Eugene, had both fought in the army, but only Eddie survived. His father, Clarence, absent during the birth descriptions in the prologue, has also died of drinking and a heart condition. The house is devoid of men: upon Eddie's return, his mother is ill, elderly, and embittered, and his sister Bette is her caretaker. Eddie is greeted by Brother, his best friend, and the two return to Eddie's home briefly to let his mother know he has arrived. She rejects them, however, and they go off to a local forest that houses homeless men (the "Bums' Forest," a recurrent site in Wideman's work). Eddie's and Brother's memories come alive there, and through a combination of storytelling and interior monologue, the reader begins to understand the nature of Eddie's crises. The dead weeds and mechanical nature of the landscape are emphasized, and Eddie witnesses a dark vision, which he calls a "shadow." He feels somehow that he is falling into it. The forest becomes his unconscious mind, and he clearly feels guilt about having survived his elder brother. He also expresses pain born of a dearth of love from his father. Brother, who is loyal and not judgmental, provides the comfort his family does not.

The first section of the novel also introduces Thurley, a despondent alcoholic who can only lecture to his students after taking a drink. The counterpart to his ongoing despair comes in multiple forms: his drinking, his collection of antiques, his enjoyment of classical music, and especially his affairs with young black men. Part of what motivates Thurley is a neurotic form of racial anxiety. After his assignation with a nameless black boy, he writes in his diary, "Consummation—the momentary reconciliation of black and white in the heat of coition" (40). When he meets Eddie, who holds him in immediate contempt and orders him away from Brother, Thurley claims, "I haven't come to prey on him. . . . We wound up together because I'm like him." Eddie, however, has a different interpretation: "you're hungry and the price of nigger meat is cheap" (50). Brother defends Thurley and reinforces his hopeful belief that race does not stand in the way of closeness. These three characters—one white, one black, and one with both black and white features—represent three distinct points of view that are initially difficult to reconcile. Wideman focuses on all three, but especially on Eddie and Thurley, both of whom are infected with some kind of poison, the origins of which are initially unclear.

Allusions to Eliot's *The Waste Land* arise frequently in Thurley's sections, indicating the poem's crises: humanity has become mechanical, a lack of fertility connects to a widespread spiritual malaise, and there might not be any resurrection after death nor any redemption after suffering. All these motifs surface as Thurley visits his friend Al to attend a church service on Easter. Prior to going, they drink gin and reflect on their shared history. We learn that Thurley, the last male heir of an aristocratic southern family, had been married to Eleanor, who has gone mad. He traces her madness to a drunken night in Italy when Al joined them in a wild threesome. This stark realization of the end of innocence forces the couple in opposite directions: "Her moving steadily toward wanton insanity and me creeping back on my hands and knees to little boys" (88). The fact that these boys tend to be black has to do with his southern heritage, as revealed in a short but telling memory of his black nanny, Hattie—"the model for Aunt Jemima Thurley always thought of her later, bustling and black with that half anxious, half smiling moon of a face peering down at him, always going straight to the root of whatever he was feeling" (72–73). Thurley's desperate trysts with young black boys can be interpreted as an attempt to return to his own youth and to reconcile his deeply troubled mind with the person who could get to "the root of whatever he was feeling." His conscience plagues him throughout this section, causing guilt about his relationship with Eleanor and Al and what they did in bed on that fateful night in Italy. His flight from Hattie in this short remembered scene initiates a need to overcome his distance from her in terms of race, gender, and social class.

Eddie's return home for Easter is driven by his need to reconcile both with his mother and with his former lover, Alice. Memories continue to weigh on him, and he longs to return to a preserved past: "He hoped so badly Alice would be home, that like Brother she would be waiting unchanged, even in the same clothes, as if time were never more than the space between a glance away and back" (105). This quotation, which provides the novel's title, represents Eddie's awareness that circumstances have changed, coupled with his foolish nostalgia for a past that contained suffering and pain, some of which he caused. Eddie also tries to reconnect with his sister Bette, who has squandered her young adulthood caring for their mother. At first Eddie can think of nothing to say to his sister, but when Bette tells him how excited she is to have him back for Easter, he becomes animated, for Easter is the day his grandfather took him to see the sanctified dance and sing. Eddie's storytelling creates a vital space for the siblings to bond. This joy of storytelling and listening is short-lived, though, as Eddie realizes that he has worked to erase his past but that his mother has not. He urges Bette to run away, insisting that their mother will survive. Their mother has been listening to the conversation, and her response is to topple down the stairs to her death but only after pointing her crutches at Eddie and smiling, creating an image he will never be able to erase. He again runs from his house, screaming this time.

The death of Eddie's mother propels him not only out of his house but into his memory. He recalls his time at the asylum, a place that felt like a prison even though he was technically free to leave whenever he wished. In a letter to his mother and sister sent just before he returns for Easter, he pleads for their support: “Deep inside there is only screaming, that or a dull, smothering silence. After we reach that deep, the only hope is to see a hand, or hear a quiet voice, anything outside that can be believed, that is as real as the madness” (138). This is the condition he is in when he returns home, and the events on Easter do not lead to any such belief. He returns, desperately, to the church where he and his grandfather had once witnessed the joy of dancing, but all he encounters now is a belligerent wino and gathering mourners. Thurley attends a different church at the same time but is driven out of it by his own brand of madness—alcoholism. The second section of the novel ends with both protagonists aware of the persistence of their troubled pasts but unable to move past them. Thurley senses rain coming, but it is far from a cleansing rain: the petals on the trees he sees “would float, mixing with the scum and acrid green to form mottled rainbows in stagnant pools” (145).

The short third section of the novel brings together its three principle figures: Eddie, Thurley, and Brother meet in a mostly black bar where Eddie and Brother have gone to score drugs and Thurley has gone to seek company. As with their earlier meeting, there is extreme antagonism between Eddie and Thurley even though they both suffer from a similar kind of self-destructive affliction born of guilt. After much tense conversation, Thurley attempts to heal Eddie by confessing ideas he has spent much time formulating but kept largely inside himself: “The spirit can’t live on air, and especially the air that’s inside our bodies. It flourishes when it touches other things—people, work” (166). Eddie mocks him: “You say you think you understand. The spirit needs this, needs that. . . . Some people, the black ones you see around you, they live without spirit” (167). Thurley tries to convince him that the substance he is seeking in this bar will not cure him, that they have to leave together and get through this night. It is Eddie who stands up and leads the threesome out, and Brother’s voice takes over. He does not know where Eddie is leading them: at first they go to the Sanctified church, but they keep going, eventually ending up on a rock in the Bums’ Forest.

The novel’s ending is masterful and mysterious: the voices of all three characters overlap in interior monologues. In symbolic contrast to *The Waste Land*–like rain predicted throughout the novel, Brother builds a fire to warm them. All three confront their separate demons as the flames burn and grow, and it is unclear by the novel’s conclusion whether the flames will consume them or simply reignite their will to live. Brother has the last word, speaking for all three of them as he expresses fascination with the fire and curiosity about what it feels like: “*I can understand why kids do it cause I want to touch myself just like one I want to put my hand in I want to go to smoke and see how high . . .*”

(186). In a novel filled with pain, this final image is one of transcendence, but it comes at a price.

To say that *A Glance Away* is a complex first novel is to understate the case considerably. Its focused, relentless emotional intensity and its Faulknerian methodology combine to make it a rich introduction to Wideman's work. A review in the *New York Times* described it as "tight, compact, and shining with verbal and dramatic skill," proclaiming Wideman to be "a novelist of high seriousness and depth."[5] Despite its praise, the review reveals dated expectations of what black literature should be, focusing excessively on the novel's minor concerns with drug addiction. In a recent article Keith Byerman argued that the novel's lack of critical attention might also have to do with its homoerotic content, which has proven "troublesome for black critical discourse."[6] For Guzzio, critical inattention to this work is the starting point of a misreading of Wideman's works in general, as critics have failed to see the complex hybridity of his work, instead labeling it "Eurocentric in one period or Afrocentric in another."[7]

Regardless of this debate, the poetry of T. S. Eliot connects Wideman's first novel to his second, *Hurry Home.* Wideman has admitted that Thurley in *A Glance Away* "resembles Prufrock,"[8] and the same can be observed of Charles Webb in *Hurry Home:* at one point Webb walks "along the [Spanish] beach dreaming a Prufrock dream of himself" (99). He even rolls up his trousers, just as Eliot's sad protagonist does. Wideman has claimed that his early novels were an attempt to "hook" the world of black experience "into what I thought was something that would give those situations and people a kind of literary resonance, legitimize that world by infusing echoes of T. S. Eliot" and other "Continental masters."[9] Although the black characters in the first two novels are not exempt from allusions to Eliot, it is these two lonely, aging white characters—Thurley and Webb—who explicitly evoke "The Love Song of J. Alfred Prufrock," a poem that turns world weariness and the fear of death into a full-blown existential crisis laced with paralysis and anguish. Yet the solitary malaise of Eliot's character spreads out and connects to the culture all around him, and so the angst of these characters touches all the characters in the books: isolation is not exclusively a white man's disease. Wideman explained that his early novels "share some of Eliot's vision. . . . one of the themes that Eliot is dealing with is cultural collapse."[10]

In *Hurry Home* part of this cultural collapse is signaled by the thwarted career dreams of its central character, Cecil Otis Braithwaite. Cecil has a law degree but works as a janitor. The novel opens with a scene of futile anger and barren decay: Cecil crushes an empty can and reflects on the fact that it and all the other garbage has to "go down" (3). This descent of garbage mirrors his own decline: on the first page we learn that he is often drunk in the morning, that he cries and curses when no one else is around, that he creates extra work for himself by throwing tenants' garbage down the stairs, that he suffers from hemorrhoids, that the sight of his resulting blood "depresses" him "with thoughts of death and dissolution" (3), and that he has hit his wife on multiple occasions. The cultural collapse Wideman sees in Eliot is Cecil's world. The questions the novel asks include: how did he get to this point? Is there any hope for salvation? Is dreaming a way of avoiding or escaping reality, or is it a way of reshaping and interpreting one's reality? On this first page Cecil's dreaming is given that sort of power: "Some mornings Cecil dreamed while he carted, but sometimes he thought black thoughts and handled the trash bags as if he could hurt them" (3). The novel ends with the sentence, "So Cecil dreamed" (185). The fact that the novel is framed by dreams and that it is characterized by imaginative flights of fancy destabilizes it to the point that it is nearly impossible to discuss "reality" in the novel; Guzzio even wonders whether the novel's basic events—Cecil's travels—actually happen: "Time has no structure in dreams. It is possible, even likely, that Braithwaite never actually travels to Europe or Africa."[11] The central symbol in the novel is Hieronymus Bosch's famous painting "The Garden of Earthly Delights," a nightmarish work of early surrealism. The painting haunts Cecil and seems to hold the key to his understanding of the world, though he cannot articulate its meaning. The fact that the painting hangs in the Prado Museum in Madrid does indicate that Cecil's travels are real, though the chronology of his life is rendered deliberately unclear.

The novel begins with this one very tangible action: Cecil crushes a can on November 14, 1968, and drops it five flights, creating an echoing clatter. The response to this action is what opens up the novel: "In another world Cecil heard a door opening. A shadow flitted across his silence, then the light footfall of a voice. *Why did you do that,* once, twice, and perhaps again" (4). The voice may be imagined, or it may be real, as Cecil attributes it to a white woman with red hair who lives in a fourth-floor apartment. She may be his lover or the object of a sexual fantasy. The fact that her voice originates "in another world" blurs this line but also signals Cecil's alienation. The novel attempts to understand his alienation, to ask questions of his profound aloneness and the significance of his actions. "Why did you do that?" is repeated throughout the book. Wideman said of this repetition, "I hope that 'Why did you do that?' has a symphonic effect, that it accrues meaning with each instance. At first it might be the very specific question of why he threw the can down the steps; but it is also 'Why did you go to law school?' 'Why did you go to Europe?' 'Why did you go to Africa?' 'Why have you chosen the kind of life you've chosen?' I hope that this question spirals."[12] The novel penetrates the surface of reality to search for deeper understanding, just as Bosch's dreamlike painting represents complex layers of human imagining.

The theme of strained or broken patrilineal relationships is a pervasive one in Wideman's work. In *Hurry Home* it manifests itself in Cecil's mourning over his stillborn son, Simon, in Webb's yearnings for his lost son, and in the relationship between Webb and Cecil as an attempt to substitute for these yearnings. The novel reveals the fact of Cecil's stillborn son gradually, but the first scene is redolent with imagery that suggests it: lifeless leaves fall from trees in this season of death, women in his building leave used tampons "atop the trash cans in full view" (5), and Cecil recalls once listening to Esther's womb: "That was early when we believed and there was some point in stopping and listening. There is no point now asking me *why*. . . . Might as well ask why I died inside her" (8). The death of his son represents for Cecil the death of his spirit, his belief, his love of Esther, and understanding of his own meaning. The crisis of the novel is that these deaths have cut off Cecil's belief in explanation: in a novel that persistently asks, "Why?" there is this troubling nihilism: "There is no point now asking me *why*."

Further complicating Cecil's nihilism is the fact that Esther believes that "Cecil would be her salvation" (9). Her belief is at odds with his lack of belief. She sees his November moods as a trial for her to overcome, but she privately wrestles with fear and doubt. The difference may be that Cecil has forced himself to confront the abyss of human existence repeatedly—symbolized again through the nightmarish Bosch painting—whereas Esther clings to her hope of a better afterlife. It could be said that Esther is a religious believer who is privately skeptical, while Cecil is an unbeliever who clings to a need to believe despite the depths of his despair.

Cecil feels some guilt as he tells his life story in conjunction with Esther's, acknowledging that his success in law school is directly linked to the sacrifices she has made. He conceives of her as a maternal figure as much as a wife: "Esther Brown, true avatar of that selfless, sore-kneed mother every night scrubbing the halls bright so next morning second generation son could tall stride the shining corridors" (13). He imagines that she calls him "my sleepyhead baby" (14), further confusing his identity with that of his stillborn son. In a letter to her, he offers his explanations for why he has left her. It is at this point that the novel disrupts all conventions, especially of time; Cecil writes, "If someone asked me the date I would look at a mirror, if someone asked me who I was I would want to see a calendar" (15). The confusion of time and his reflection in a mirror give way to a deeper identity search, one connected to his understanding of his racial difference as a child and his search for representations of black figures in Bosch's paintings in a library as an adult. Cecil wanders through lonely streets and witnesses a funeral, then recalls waking next to Esther and perceiving that she is dead. He is left with the lyrics of a spiritual, "Farther Along," which recurs throughout Wideman's works, especially the line "Farther along we'll understand why" (22). Despite the fact that these lyrics follow his horrific vision of his wife's death, they provide a modicum of hope for understanding sometime in the future.

Cecil's sexual fantasies of the red-haired woman and his daydreams about his dead son lead him to an extended meditation on Easter, the feast of resurrection, the opposite season of the dying fall that has depressed him. The closeness of Esther's name with Easter is not coincidental. He associates her with both death (Simon) and resurrection, which takes the form of memory: Simon can be brought back only in Cecil's imagination. His private life thus becomes his reality and he regards himself as the very agent of double lives: "Cecil Cecil: neither of others, libra, seesaw, see soul, sees all" (28). This Joycean riff reveals the complex nature of Cecil's existence and explains how it is possible for him to dwell on his guilty, sinful private life while Esther regards him as her path to salvation. He recalls his graduation from law school with guilt, since Esther has been working overtime to help pay for it, and rather than celebrating his achievement, he meditates on his own death in cold, automatized, corporate terms: "And in that room where all our cards are filed does some lugubrious arm in a solemn arc glide over the metal trays till it comes to B then Br then Bra and so on till it has located on Braithwaite, Cecil Otis, then delicately descend, clamp my card in its pincers, raise me, retract the arc backward till I am suspended over the proper heap of other numbers up. Drops me" (29). The passage recalls Cecil's initial act of dropping the can: he is like garbage, empty, used up. A black man who fails to achieve his dreams of becoming a lawyer, he links this fear directly to the Middle Passage, which carried slaves from Africa to the New World: "I remember the sun sudden in my eyes, the salt air too rich after the fetid hole below decks" (29). This is not to say that Cecil is incapable of succeeding in America solely because of his race but rather that his mind-set is affected by the historical atrocity of slavery.

In a telling memory Cecil is walking from his graduation, the day before his wedding, to get his hair cut, having borrowed money for that purpose from a fellow graduate. Along the way to the barber, his separation from the black community becomes evident. Cecil only has enough money for a haircut, but a shoeshine boy offers to polish his shoes for free "just cause you gonna be something someday and maybe you remember Shine" (33). This is part of the boy's hustle, though: others on the street intervene and demand that Cecil pay him, as the boy claims he never promised Cecil free work. The story is passed around the community, with Cecil rendered as the uppity "magistrate" who thinks he is better than others; the storyteller says he feels a little sorry for Cecil, who is punched and robbed of his haircut money. Cecil is damned and doomed to failure, less from his own behavior than from the circumstances of his life.

The second part of the book begins with Cecil floating back over the ocean, reversing the Middle Passage imagery from earlier, but to Europe rather than Africa. Outside the Prado museum in Madrid, he discusses with Webb both art and the similarities between Webb's black son and Cecil. Webb says, "like him you've decided to wrap yourself in old sorrows. . . . The word bitter keeps wanting to be said, but I'm sure saying it about you or him would only be another way of turning my back" (44–45). In this way Cecil is similar to Eddie from *A Glance Away* in that both dwell on personal and historical "old sorrows." Webb has brought Cecil to Europe to see the Bosch painting, and Cecil becomes fixated on a painting of a black king: one of the Magi from the Bible, who brings gifts to the infant Jesus. Cecil embodies contradictions when it comes to belief and religion, and he functions again as the source of salvation for someone else as Webb turns to him almost desperately to fill in the gap left by his own absent son. The men separate, promising to meet in six days in southern Spain at a festival, and Cecil departs on an individual quest: "Don Cecil, undertaker of perilous journey, seeker of knowledge" (48). This knowledge is an inquiry into art and history as well as the Moorish or "gypsy" culture that may hold the key to his own identity. He is anxious that he will not fully understand the art he views in the Prado without a guide: "Is there a guide for me, will one come along who knows how I must withhold my assent until I translate any language into that black subterranean one which is my own" (50). The adjective "subterranean" reinforces the novel's emphasis on descent. One of the novel's movements is back and forth across time and space, but another, just as important, is a perpetual journey downward and upward, into the depths of consciousness and history and back to the surface of shared reality.

This movement is evident as Cecil becomes unnerved by the Bosch painting: "this order, this moment of pure insight . . . would make the nightmare world of demons and evil in which the vision existed surge forward full-blown into life" (52). Cecil attempts to stave off the demons that haunt him by drinking beer in a cafe near the museum; there he falls into a conversation with a traveling American expatriate named Albert, who introduces him to a prostitute named Estrella, a name that closely resembles Esther, further blurring the line between reality and memory/imagination. Cecil and Albert embark on a bender, which is a way for Cecil to keep Bosch's vision at bay, to blot out "the raging darkness he feared in himself" (53). Despite his overt quest to forget, he continues to dwell on "older sorrows," and his visions of the Middle Passage become more vivid as he sees black bodies being thrown overboard to lighten the load of the slave ship. The scene ends with a stream-of-consciousness montage of past lovers, including Esther, interspersed with visions of decay and an abortion, and Cecil desires relief from his overactive mind.

Cecil embarks on another sea journey, this one precisely dated—April 1966—but more fantastical than the last. He is sailing toward Africa, but the continent does not appear when it should. His explicit purpose is to cross "the sea to see where it all came from. . . . He has promised to wash his hands and feet, to cry out impurities from his eyes before he touches the African soil" (114). The journey promises historical renewal or retribution for sins. His story becomes conflated with that of Tarik the Moor, the eighth-century Moroccan general who invaded Spain. Time lurches again, and Cecil decides to seek a job in Constance Beauty's hair salon rather than use his law degree to launch a career: "Cecil would make it. Jive his way through one set of real and one set of false teeth" (115). "Making it" is a way of surviving through jiving or, in other words, allowing his identity to be malleable so he is not pinned down. This decision comes with a psychological consequence, however, as he seems doomed to constant motion on a sea voyage with no end. Africa never appears.

The novel's third section begins with Esther, who is writing her alliterative memoirs with the help of a dictionary. The piled-up words seem like gibberish, but they end with the novel's title: "Hurry home, hurry home" (119). There is an urgency, at least in Esther's mind, for Cecil to complete his quest and return to her. Her writing turns into a canonization of him, for she believes that her salvation and his, following a lifetime of suffering, are interdependent, a "twined destiny" (122). She addresses God directly, interpreting her own anger at the loss of her son and departure of her husband as a weak loss of faith, and interpreting Cecil's exile as a necessary quest for enlightenment. She also believes that the routine sexual adventures of her own adolescence are part of God's grand design, which will help her identify Cecil as a chosen saint. Her relationship with God, with her father, and with Cecil could all be described as masochistic: she understands their love through punishment. Thus Cecil's abandonment of her is evidence of his close association with God.

Her memoir is dated April 19, 1967, and the rest of the novel is composed of Cecil's journal, dating from March 2 through April 19. Much of the journal is devoted to his relationship with Esther, including his near obsession with the death of Simon. This event is so traumatic that it nearly prevents his ability to love and to understand the essence of his identity. Another large section of the journal is devoted to his recollection of his uncle's version of the story of Tarik the Moor. A much fuller version of the story, this rendition reinforces the importance of family in transmitting culture. This point is made ironic in Cecil's return to Simon as the subject of the last, longest entry in his journal, on

April 19. He gradually reveals that November, his season of sorrow, is actually when Simon was conceived, and that his end came in the spring, the traditional season of renewal. Wideman uses the opportunity to allude yet again to Eliot's *The Waste Land,* which famously begins, "April is the cruelest month." In Cecil's case the cruelty of April originated in November: "in my desperation death brought you forth. . . . Simon, can you ever forgive" (151). Cecil's guilt, which leads to his self-loathing, his bouts of hedonism, and his inability to stay true to Esther, is tied up with the unfulfilled promise of life. The fact that he feels responsible for this accident of nature testifies to his incurable feeling that he is doomed, regardless of his actions. As he says to his unborn son, "No, the black man was not meant to be. Ask them, any of them. *You are not real.* And unless some God comes down and starts to kissing this black clay again it will crumble and blow away ungrieved, unfollowed, and without remorse" (153). His solution to this dilemma is to embrace his work as a hairdresser, a job that no longer separates him from his community, as when he was Magistrate Cecil, but also makes him "Creator of an art that has no past or future, no tradition to be sustained or transmitted infinitesimally modified to generations unborn" (162). His final gesture is an attempt at storytelling, which always represents the potential for healing in Wideman's works. Cecil tells his own story to his Uncle Otis, bridging the gap between generations and forcing Cecil to become the interpreter and chronicler of his own life. He tries to explain why he left Esther, how his desire for knowledge of his own origins sent him out of his own life and onto a journey. Otis, in turn, passes along stories and visions to his nephew in further attempts to make sense of origins and death. Cecil finally resolves to turn from this oracle and to return to Esther, and the novel's pattern of departure and return is complete. He is both the Prodigal Son and Odysseus: "He was home again, he would be welcomed" (184).

The *New York Times* review of *Hurry Home* acknowledged Wideman's gifts as a storyteller—calling the novel "immensely rich and complicated"—but also suggested that the richness and complication might go too far: "At times the [literary] devices seem a thicket through which one must hack one's weary way toward meanings arbitrarily obscure."[13] Coleman saw the novel as a failure, like *A Glance Away,* because it does not "combine mainstream modernism and black tradition in a way that would produce a black voice."[14] Guzzio did not see the novel as a failure for that reason and instead analyzed it as an extended meditation on DuBois's concept of double-consciousness.[15]

Despite the critical tendency to classify Wideman's first three novels together and to distinguish them from his later work, *The Lynchers* (1973) is more of a departure from the first two works than such a classification allows. It relies less on modernist techniques such as stream-of-consciousness monologues, and allusions to Eliot, Joyce, and Faulkner are not evident. The novel is built on voices, sometimes in dialogue and sometimes in interior monologue. Moreover, the collective subject of the title indicates a move toward a collective consciousness. *A Glance Away* and *Hurry Home* focus mainly on a single protagonist who is aloof and alienated. *The Lynchers* describes a damaged community who create a misguided plot to address the wrongs of history. Four acquaintances—Willie Hall (also known as Littleman), Graham Rice, Lenny Saunders, and Thomas Wilkerson—devise a plan to murder a black prostitute named Sissie and lynch the white police officer who is her pimp. The men pin their identities to the success or failure of this plan, suggesting the futility of vengeful crime as a response to racial injustice and historical atrocities.

The novel begins with a lengthy list of those atrocities, including over one hundred lynchings in a three-year period from 1868 to 1871, almost exactly one hundred years before the novel takes place. Wideman titled this section "Matter Prefatory," and its existence is presented by the author neutrally for the reader's interpretation: the characters in the novel never refer to this history, though they are its heirs. The novel proper opens not with "the lynchers" but with Thomas Wilkerson's parents. His father Orin wakes up with a hangover and encounters his ruined world. Images of decay and poverty permeate his apartment, and he transfers his dissatisfaction to his wife, telling her to buy a new robe to replace the tattered one she wears. This is just the first instance in the novel of black people misdirecting their anger at one another.

Orin Wilkerson sits with his friend Childress at a bar, listening to him brag about his sexual exploits. The scene is crude and lengthy, but the stories eventually open up the space for Orin to meditate on the mystical qualities of jazz. The novel opens with Orin dreaming of himself as a musician, and in this scene he thinks, "maybe jazz dreaming too" (39). This music offers a transcendent alternative to the decay and poverty around him, and it also offers the possibility of deep connection to another person or community, one that Childress's loveless sexual encounters do not provide. Orin works as a garbage collector, one paid to take care of the waste left behind by humanity, only to see it resurface daily. At work he meditates on the incomprehensibility of the Charles Manson murders, trying to figure out, along with his coworkers, the sickness that would lead to such an act: "you take all the pieces and it still don't add up" (46). The historical atrocities in the "Matter Prefatory," the plot to kill Sissie and lynch the white police officer, and Orin's murder of his "main man" Childress later in the novel testify to the fact that the same sickness pervades Orin's world. As Childress says of their decrepit garbage truck, "The mothafuckas gonna come clean apart one of these days" (48). His prediction might apply to his culture in general.

The novel then shifts to three of "the lynchers": Littleman, Saunders, and Thomas Wilkerson. Thomas notices a persistent edginess as they discuss the plan. Littleman is clearly the ringleader and architect of the scheme; Saunders is ready to act but resentful of Littleman's authority; and Thomas is reluctant, "unable to see the plan except as a joke or enormous threat" (49). Saunders and Littleman, who prove the most impulsive and violent of the group, play a variation on "the dozens," insulting each other and pushing one another past the limits of tolerance. Littleman denigrates the tradition of the dozens, ascribing the game to "some darky" who "had nothing better to do than insult the fool darky lying next to him in Mr. Charlie's hog pen" (49). Saunders, referring to Littleman's physical handicap, retorts by calling him "a sorry assed, runty nigger who don't like hisself" (50). As in the first scenes with Orin Wilkerson, there is an underlying tension here involving racial self-loathing and the tendency to lash out at one's friends and loved ones. These tendencies are clearly a deep-seated cancer in the black community caused by the historical atrocities listed in the "Matter Prefatory."

The novel exploits the ways individuals interpret and create their reality. The central conceit of the book is the lynching "plot" (as it is referred to repeatedly), and much of the book's action depends upon the way this plot is conceived, imagined, reimagined, negotiated, and interpreted by the lynchers. Wideman might be riffing on his tendency to write novels with loose, unconventional plots that are the framework for characters to reveal their inner lives. The rhetoric of 1960s-era Black Nationalism is in the air, and the fourth member of the group, the reclusive, volatile Graham Rice, has partly bought into this rhetoric and combined it with his own idiosyncratic interpretations of language. He even interprets his own name at length: "he had decoded these bare outlines of a plot: that rice was the sustenance of the poor man, the oppressed; that it was white because it came from the white man, the crumbs from his table, so much lotus for blacks and Chinamen to fight over while in fact both groups were themselves being consumed by the white devils' trickery" (51–52). As though this rumination is a prophecy, the other three lynchers burst into his apartment, and while dividing up the chicken that was supposed to sustain Rice for the next few days, Rice finds himself taking more than his share not only of the chicken but also of the beer and marijuana the others have brought to the impromptu feast, just so that Saunders will not have it. Meanwhile, Littleman and Thomas challenge each other to arm wrestling. The jazz they play on the record player again provides a contrast to their petty competitions with one another, providing the model of an art form that is cooperative even as it allows soloists to display their individuality.

Littleman not only conceives of the lynching plot but also interprets its significance: "Divides the world simple and pure. Good or bad. Oppressors and oppressed. Black or white. Things tend to get a little fuzzy here in the big city. We need ritual" (60). Although simplicity has popular appeal, it is suspect in Wideman's work, which embraces artistic and intellectual complexity. Littleman's fantasies about the nature of the world are dynamic but primitive. "Power must always be absolute," he says. "When it's not absolute it's something weaker. . . . You must be prepared to assert your power brutally and arbitrarily if it is to remain pure" (61). This rhetoric is at odds with his theory that their act will divide the world, for they (the oppressed) are aiming to become oppressors. The ritual, in other words, will muddle the lines Littleman talks about rather than clarify them.

The ritual is more powerful in its conception than it could ever become in reality. There is a distinct emphasis on language in this section and on the way the lynchers use language to create a story—a parallel to Childress's stories of sexual conquest, which also contain more than a little fantasy. Thomas is anxious as he senses that their words are actually leading them toward action, and he continues to come to terms with Littleman's words even after he leaves the group. Littleman's fiery speeches echoing in Thomas's head are "hard and brittle like sleet in the chill air" (66); he wishes for jazz music to cancel them out, but none is available. He is rattled by Littleman's words, and he is at a vulnerable crossroads in his life, aware of his failings and mediocrity and disgusted by "the poverty and downfall of his family" (68). He is the alienated intellectual type first presented in Wideman's first two novels but is more impressionable than the others, and although it is not solely "his" novel, the choices he makes have significant consequences on the outcome. He is, like Thurley in *A Glance Away,* a jaundiced schoolteacher with a problematic relationship to alcohol. As he prepares to teach, he reflects on time and fate, staring a calendar on which he has marked the day of the lynching. The calendar looks logical, but as he contemplates it, he begins to doubt the efficacy of Littleman's plan. He is motivated by a desire to live a life that is not his father's, but he is wary of the anarchy that the plan will unleash. He is also curious about his own ability to create something artistic, and doubts Littleman's claims to be a poet. His ambivalence is clear as he tries to instill in his fifth-graders—all black—a sense of African pride, while privately reflecting on his own embarrassing encounter with the first African he met, or the way he hid his dashiki under white cotton shirts. He tells his students that they are "heirs of [Africa's] legacy," but silently wonders if he should have said "victims" instead of heirs (83).

Thomas recalls a night when he wore his dashiki and styled his hair in an Afro, largely to impress Tanya, his coworker with whom he is in love. He had invited her to his parents' apartment for dinner. Before she arrives, his mother browbeats him, punishing him for her discontentment with her impoverished, thankless life. She scoffs at his declaration of love, saying, "Time and poor and hate and hurt I know something about, but I don't know love" (95). Orin arrives home, predictably drunk, and the couple engage in an embarrassing fight in front of Thomas as well as Tanya, who witnesses the ugly scene through an open door. This unfortunate event sends Thomas in pursuit of Tanya, but he pauses, paralyzed, and thinks deeply about their predicament. His horror at the prospect of living his parents' routine life without the possibility for improvement leads to a nightmarish fantasy about the lives of black people in his building. He imagines the building as "doomed" and its residents as cogs in a huge machine that is on the verge of exploding and raining dust all around. He takes flight, terrified, and it is clear that his ambivalence about the lynching plan is bound to this moment of revelation.

The novel's second section begins with Littleman watching a game of basketball, which functions like music or like Thomas's furtive belief in love: as an alternative to the nihilistic ritual of the lynching. Despite his physical handicap, Littleman is "not jealous" of the players because their play enables him to feel "his crippled legs high stepping up an invisible ladder toward the sun" (110). He meets Thomas and lectures him about playground basketball and about the eighteenth-century architecture of downtown Philadelphia. He interprets the Age of Reason as an age of delusion that masked the true reality of early America, which was built on the suffering of slaves. His desire, through enacting the lynching, is to tear down this society and to let others figure out how to build it back up: "let tomorrow take care of itself" (110). Although Littleman's rhetoric is persuasive, Thomas remains skeptical because he wants to believe in love and beauty, and because he feels the need only to figure out his own life. Littleman is not focused on individuals, but his vision of groups is distorted. He claims, "We will lynch one man but in fact we will be denying a total vision of reality" (116). In terms of black people, he overlooks some key moments in the history of black liberation as he seeks to enact his plan: "When have we ever risen up as a people, united, resolved ready to die together. Never, never once in our pitiful history" (116). The righteousness of his anger is clouded by a flawed logic that denies both the past and the future and yet also declares the sovereignty of the black nation. He claims to Wilkerson, "the plan's as simple as death" (117), not acknowledging that death is not simple at all. His rhetoric is fiery and persuasive, involving nationhood and self-sacrifice, but it is also terrifying in the way it negates individual lives and significance.

It is ironic, then, that when Littleman puts the first phase of his plan into action, he is nameless and powerless, referred to by the police as a "crazy black dwarf" (121). He has delivered an incendiary speech on the front steps of a middle school, and the police react with an excessive show of force, dragging Littleman off to a hospital and psych ward where he remains for the rest of the novel. His backstory is revealed, beginning with his humiliation in an encounter with a prostitute who robs him and followed by his first meeting with Angela, his lover, who approaches him as he spends time alone on a beach at night. The history of their relationship intensifies his feelings of inadequacy as he is turned away from every job for which he applies. He recalls all this from the hospital room where he drifts in and out of consciousness while the other lynchers comment on his condition. Thomas summons enough courage to overcome his self-loathing and speaks as the self-appointed new leader of the group. He sees a new version of himself arising: "this new unfamiliar version of Thomas Wilkerson, so direct, so forceful was a wonder, but a wonder betrayed even as he metamorphosed from the ashes of the old. . . . Action, thought, both still born. But one gets you out of a room, onto the street, bumps you into other human beings" (146–147).

The tension between thought and action informs the entire novel. Saunders, a man more given to action than thought, is the foil to Thomas, whose tendency to analyze impedes his capacity for action. Like the others, Saunders has a troubled background. Specifically, he comes from a broken family: his mother is insane and poor, and all his siblings had different fathers, none of whom offered support. His contribution to the lynching plot is to murder Sissie, the prostitute who works for the white police officer who will be lynched. Littleman assuages Saunders's moral reservations about killing Sissie by arguing that she is just a pawn in the oppressor's system, but Saunders is troubled because his mother might have been described the same way. Sissie's name underscores the familial guilt he feels, suggesting that there are always connections between people that make it difficult to commit murder in the name of social progress. Empathy prevents Saunders from carrying out his plan, and it could be this feeling of kinship that reminds him of African icons as he looks at Sissie and her daughter.

Littleman, unable to act since he is confined in the hospital, is alone with his thoughts. He reveals that his only action is to write every day, but then to soak the pages in water until they are illegible and to destroy them. He considers it fitting that his thoughts will not be read: "Oblivion for my words appropriate because my people have always written their history with their mouths" (167). This acknowledgment of the importance of orality to African American history also indicates Littleman's isolation: he can no longer communicate the reasoning behind his plan even to his inner circle. His mind becomes the only repository for reality, and he uses his imagination to construct a story that will make sense of the fact that his beloved Angela left him without a word. He ascribes mythical, theological significance to his plot to lynch the police officer, believing that godliness is synonymous with attaching meaning to action: "To free the Black God I will drop the hanged cop in the fire. . . . To tear such a hole in history. To assist at the birth of a God. These are worth any sacrifice" (172, 173). Rather than keep these thoughts entirely to himself, he spends time educating a black boy named Anthony, who comes to clean his room. Part of this education involves playing power games with the workers at the hospital: Littleman wants Anthony to believe that he is in control and that their solidarity constitutes a form of power, even if it only applies to something as mundane as breaking the rules against smoking in the hospital room. He transfers his own paranoia to the boy, calling him a puppet of the white world even as he manipulates him so that he can execute the plan while in the hospital. His attitude toward the boy is dangerous and potentially harmful, but that does not matter to Littleman, who continues to think of individual lives as subordinate to the lynching plot.

The lynching plot is thrown off neither by Littleman's confinement to the hospital nor by the infighting of the lynchers, but rather because Thomas's father Orin murders his best friend over a minor drunken dispute. Thomas's visit to his father in prison is the first instance of this motif that becomes prominent in Wideman's later work. It is an affecting scene, with Orin admitting to his own stupidity and Thomas listening, dumbfounded, as his father dissolves in front of his eyes and becomes like everyone else who is locked up. He drinks in a bar after visiting his father and attempts to work through the ethical dilemmas that surround him: Was killing Sissie necessary? Had Childress's death carried any meaning? Was it fair to put the lives of countless black people in jeopardy when society retaliated for the lynching? His conclusion acknowledges the randomness of his world: "How could you form a plan in a world where all that mattered was accidental, a blind jumble of blind forces?" (213). He believes that confronting Sissie face to face will help clarify his confusion, and he recalls a conversation in which Saunders accuses him of inaction because of overthinking: "*We're past talking. We're moving*" (215). Responding in his mind to the question "What do you people want?" he concludes that black people don't just want abstract concepts like peace and dignity, but rather they want "everything. And I want it with the same hunger and ruthlessness you see in yourself" (220). Framed this way, the African American condition is one of suppressed desire that cannot be fulfilled, given the limiting circumstances of contemporary society.

Although Thomas never finds Sissie, he does come across a little girl whom he believes to be Sissie's daughter, and he feels overwhelming tenderness toward her as she sings a familiar childhood rhyme. He wonders whether he has ever taught his schoolchildren anything valuable or whether he has just suppressed their desire, which would align him with the oppressors. He visits Tanya in the middle of the night and tells her everything; she listens in silent horror, then pronounces the plan "ugly and sick" (237) despite Thomas's attempts to label Littleman a "genius" (236). Thomas's final resolve is to disrupt the plot by going to Rice, who is in charge of the guns. When Thomas knocks on his door, Rice retrieves the largest gun, aims it at the closed door, and fires. The narrative then shifts to Saunders waiting in a bar for Thomas the next morning, and the fact that Thomas does not arrive suggests that Rice's paranoid shot found its mark. Saunders is more vitriolic and offensive than ever, and since the plot is now solely in his hands, the reader understands how it has degenerated into vengeful violence, if it was ever anything more. A brief coda to Orin's story reinforces this idea as he contemplates what remains of his identity after murdering his best friend. The novel ends with Anthony, the young worker in Littleman's hospital, ruminating about his life, which echoes the lives of the lynchers: Rice's helplessness, Saunders's misogyny and racial anger, Littleman's desire for change, and Thomas Wilkerson's paralyzing analysis. He ends his rounds on the seventh floor, where the insane patients are kept, and Littleman is there, rendered mute by tranquilizers. He has always been associated with words, but now he is just a blinking, furious, inert mass of humanity. The sadness and rage in his face are pathetic, and Anthony backs slowly out of Littleman's room, completing the novel ambiguously, similar to Wideman's first two novels.

The Lynchers is lumped in with Wideman's first two novels because it was written before he took his famous hiatus to prepare himself for the Homewood Trilogy. However, *The Lynchers* really does not connect easily to the earlier books. Reviewers and critics treated it as evidence that the author they were hoping for in Wideman was beginning to emerge. A *Times* reviewer faulted Wideman for being "wordy" and claimed that the novel's structure is "shaky," but opined that "he can *write,* and you come away from the book with the feeling that he is . . . very close to getting it all together."[16] Coleman praised the book because it does not simply repeat the theme of the black intellectual's isolation from the black community: "*Lynchers* is Wideman's first book to be set entirely in the black community and to give an important place in its structure to black historical tradition, speech, and cultural tradition. Wideman still does not achieve the full, mature black voice that we find in the Homewood trilogy, however."[17] Trudier Harris, in a study of representations of lynching in novels, praised Wideman for taking "the subject of lynching beyond its gruesome brutalities to a level of philosophical reflection" and concluded that the novel is "an exploration of the desire for revenge on the part of those who lack the depravity necessary to effect that revenge."[18] Building on Harris's assessment, Ashraf Rushdy argued that "Wideman raises questions about the complexities of the past and the viability of black nationalism for the present."[19] His reading reveals Wideman as a critic of "the idea of black nationalism in order to expose those unhealthy features that are almost invariably at the heart of strategies of nation-building."[20]

The divergence between an early reading like Coleman's and a more recent one like Rushdy's may be attributable to the trajectory of Wideman's writing over time—that is, that he did not resolve the dilemma of the alienated black intellectual and his community in any permanent way—or to the expectations of certain readers at certain times. Taken together, these three novels do not present a simple, coherent statement about Wideman's understanding of race, racial identity, or the political obligations of black fiction; rather, they are about struggling against fate. In this struggle, one's imagination can provide alternatives to stark reality, but it can also be a source of torment. These concerns, coupled with deeply philosophical interests in time, art, and the ghosts of history, permeate Wideman's work. To say that these works are fundamentally different from the rest of Wideman's oeuvre is to deny the fact that all of his books are unique and that the only constant characteristic of his writing is its tireless experimentation.

CHAPTER 3

Homewood Bound

The three books that make up the Homewood Trilogy—*Damballah* (1981), *Hiding Place* (1981), and *Sent for You Yesterday* (1983)—were published in quick succession to great acclaim following Wideman's self-imposed period of retraining. Many critics have denigrated his first three novels and have praised the trilogy by contrast. The reasons for this assessment are manifold, but in general critics found the first three novels too willing to participate in white modernist traditions, making them seem insufficiently attentive to Wideman's African American heritage. Notable in this regard is James Coleman, who claimed that Wideman, in the early novels, "fails to achieve the black voice that will allow him to use modernism." From his viewpoint *The Lynchers* was a step in the right direction, but the Homewood trilogy was the true breakthrough, for there he was able to "use black speech, cultural rituals, and religious songs to express the attitudes and responses that have allowed blacks to rise above oppression and hardship and to flourish spiritually in America."[1] This assessment laid the table for many subsequent critics, and the pre-Homewood novels have been largely ignored while the Homewood books have become the standard by which his other work has been assessed. Critics have placed the Homewood books in conversation with such classics of the African American tradition as Ellison's *Invisible Man*.[2] Guzzio has argued convincingly that the division of Wideman's career into pre- and post-Homewood Trilogy limits an understanding of Wideman's oeuvre and possibly distorts the way readers approach individual works.

Regardless of how one views the Homewood Trilogy, it was conceived as a coherent unit and does mark a change in trajectory (if not a "progression" in Coleman's assessment).[3] For Guzzio these works (as well as others situated in

Homewood) "operate as a lens by which Wideman views the history of his race and the historical consciousness of America, and Wideman uses these family narratives—these stories of home—to directly refute the stories written by outsiders to describe what it means to be an African American in this country."[4] Their grand achievement is to make stories that might only seem to be interesting to a small group of people expand in their significance without making overt pronouncements about them that tie them to a broader historical pattern. Wideman had hoped that would be the case; in an important 1983 interview with Wilfred D. Samuels, he said, "I am not interested in investigating family and community in a generalized, universal context. My subject is a Black family . . . in a particular city. . . . I hope by examining the particularity of my past that I am making it exist on its own terms—but, that at the same time, giving it greater accessibility."[5]

"Accessibility" might mean general applicability in this context, but it also suggests that these works are less forbidding to readers who may be put off by Wideman's dazzling, difficult techniques. In that same interview he stated that his "number one" goal in penning the Homewood Trilogy was "to reach out to levels of audience that perhaps the earlier works had excluded." To put a finer point on it, he added, "I know my black readership is minimal. . . . If you could get the books in the same places that other consumer goods are, maybe the books can compete. . . . That is why I wrote the way I did in the last two books and published them in paperbacks. I'm hoping that maybe someday one of these books will be accessible to a wide Black audience."[6] The reader of the Homewood Trilogy still has to work hard, but in this case the hard work involves connection to context rather than laboring through densely rendered prose and allusions to works that Wideman learned (he admitted in this interview) through the "value system imposed on [him]" at Penn and Oxford.[7] That said, looking back on his career, the Homewood Trilogy did not represent a "turning point"—a phrase he and Samuels used repeatedly in this interview—so much as a temporary departure, for it would be difficult to argue that many of the post-trilogy works are as accessible as they are.

The phrase often used to describe this period is what Wideman called his need to develop his "Homewood ear" (*Brothers and Keepers* 76). As he told Samuels, "I have returned to Homewood and have sort of settled in. I am trying to listen again."[8] The pattern of exile and return is in fact the plot of *A Glance Away* and *Hurry Home,* indicating that the Homewood Trilogy is not as much of a departure as one would think, but critics latched onto the idea that Wideman admitted that he needed to "listen again" as evidence that he had stopped listening to the stories, language, and history of his people. The phrase could just as easily mean "listen a second time," however, just as "revision" implies a second look. He might be said to be listening on a deeper level in these books, but it is clear that he is listening to more voices, and to specific voices: those from his familial and ancestral past in a very specific place. *Damballah,* the first book in the trilogy, begins with a letter to his brother, a "Begat Chart," and a family tree that outlines the genealogy that is the crucial framework for this fictional inquiry.

Damballah, Wideman's first collection of short stories, enabled him to shuttle between time periods without resorting to the in-text shifts that some readers find challenging in his novels. The first two stories in the collection, "Damballah" and "Daddy Garbage," allowed him the freedom to span history, moving from an unspecified time during slavery to the early 1900s. As a pair, the stories introduce themes that Wideman would continue to develop: the crucial need for storytelling, the trauma of untimely death, and the importance of ritual (burial, in this case). "Damballah" tells the story of a stubborn old slave, Orion, who is killed by overseers after he refuses to speak English, to submit to Christian conversion, and to work to the master's satisfaction. The story presents a nameless young boy who is involved with Orion's sacrifice. Orion has identified him as "the one" who "could learn the story and tell it again" (18). He utters only one word to the boy, "Damballah," the name of the chief loa in the mythology of Haitian vodun. When the boy repeats the word in front of his aunts, he is chastised and punished, but he retains enough courage to approach Orion's corpse when no one else will, and he follows his instinctive urge to throw Orion's decapitated head in the river. The meaning of the story is obscure, but the boy's action is significant. Neither he nor Orion is named on the family tree in the book's front matter: we can assume, though, that the boy is a progenitor of Sybela Owens and that his role is to attend to the African mythology and language of his heritage rather than to conform obediently to a culture that would threaten godlike figures. The boy's name has been forgotten, but his story is significant in the collective unconscious of Homewood and its residents.

"Daddy Garbage" is the name of a dog found and named by Strayhorn, who sells Italian ices to local children. They ask him about the origin of the name, and he claims to have forgotten. A third-person narrator intervenes to tell the story of how the dog once discovered a dead infant in a garbage can. Strayhorn does not know what to do with the corpse, but he intuits that it is his responsibility, just as the boy in "Damballah" rushes to the barn following the murder of Orion without fully understanding his own actions. Strayhorn and John French bury the child, and John delivers a brief eulogy: "Don't have no stone to mark this place. And don't know your name, child. . . . But none that matters now. You your own self now" (43). Injected into this tale is the memory of

John French singing as his daughter Lizabeth gives birth. John is responsible for comforting the next generation, though not in conventional ways: he is drunk in both cases. But the transmission of values across generations persists despite (or perhaps because of) untimely death in both of these stories: they are about the survival of spirit in a hostile material world.

The next three stories in the collection all involve Lizabeth, John's mother, in one capacity or another. The first, "Lizabeth: The Caterpillar Story," begins as a dialogue between Lizabeth and her mother about the stories of John French, the patriarch at the center of so many of the Homewood stories. In this one the child Lizabeth eats a tiny bite of a caterpillar, and John French's response is to eat the rest of it in solidarity. This grotesque communion connects father and daughter in a deep way, bonding them to the point that John's absences and eventual death will lead to great sorrow. She becomes anxious for the loss of her father long before she should and even feels herself disintegrating: "One part had a Daddy and loved him more than anything but the other part could see him dead or dying or run away forever and see Lizabeth alone and heartbroken or see Lizabeth lying awake all night foolish enough to think she might save her Daddy" (55). This anxiety originates from her father's threat to kill the man who is dumping ashes into the lot next to their house where he plans to grow vegetables. The caterpillar story is about sacrifice and protection, and it is reinforced when Lizabeth's mother smashes her fist through a window as a warning to John, who is being pursued by a man with a gun. The threat of death is everywhere in the story, and the family bond is both a way to stave off death and the explanation for why death matters so intensely to these characters.

In "Hazel," Lizabeth is the one who provides comfort to her traumatized relatives. Hazel, Lizabeth's cousin, is overprotected by her reclusive mother, Gaybrella. Gay's sister Bess attempts to lure her out of the apartment to come to church, warning her not to do laundry again that day, but Gay is determined to stay in her apartment, presumably to avoid the dangers of the world outside. This logic is flawed, as tragedy can strike anywhere, and it has already struck the house when Faun, one of Hazel's two brothers, pushed her down the stairs when she was seventeen, rendering her immobile for life. On the day the story takes place, Hazel dreams of staircases. Not unlike Lizabeth in the previous story, tragedy strikes again while Hazel is daydreaming: her mother's long hair and housecoat catch on fire, and she hurtles out of the third-story apartment landing, plunging to her death. Hazel dies one year later, but the story ends with Lizabeth visiting the infirm, exiled Faun in a nursing home fifteen years later. Her duty to him is simple: "She was there because Faun was Gaybrella's son and Hazel's brother and she had stopped by all those Sundays and was one of the few who remembered the whole story" (79). She imagines that his last garbled words are "Forgive me," but his atonement for his part in his sister's misfortune is almost less important than Lizabeth's steady sense of familial duty and recognition of the importance of preserving stories.

The emphasis on storytelling is underscored and highlighted when the voice of the author breaks through in the next story, "The Chinaman." The title refers to a figure who portends death in African American vernacular games and stories, and death is again pervasive in this tale in three forms: John French's ignoble demise in his bathroom, Freeda French's death, and Lizabeth's near death in a snowstorm, rescued by her aunt May. Storytelling is a way to stave off existential dread, "that dark, empty tunnel [that] is her life" (59). Storytelling converts that dark, empty tunnel to "a door opening on something clear and bright" (60). Sensing the same truth, John returns with his family to share stories of his grandmother Freeda three months after her death. For John, the stories do not have the power to conjure up reality when he is away from Homewood; on the road trip home, he finds himself whispering pathetically in the dark. He tries telling stories to his wife, but they feel "stiff, incomplete" (93) without the proper storytellers and circumstances. Once he returns, his mother tells the story of a ghostly Chinaman portending the death of Freeda. John acknowledges the difference between his attempts and his mother's: "My mother has told it, finished it like I never can. And the shape of the story is the shape of my mother's voice" (94). This is a formative moment in the evolution of Wideman's aesthetic as he fully realizes the connection between voice and story, and as he admits that his central challenge as a writer is to capture those voices faithfully in print. It is also a cogent example of how stories are intensified through their retelling, which explains the recurrence of many plots, characters, and motifs throughout his work.

"The Watermelon Story" is one of Wideman's most fully realized stories about storytelling. There are actually two watermelon stories in it: one a traumatic account of a "wino" who loses his arm after crashing through a plate-glass window in a grocery store after slipping on watermelons, the other an old fertility tale from Africa told by Aunt May. There is initially an unnamed witness to the first watermelon story: "The first time he saw somebody get their arm chopped off was in front of the A & P on Homewood Avenue" (99). As the story continues, we learn that this boy had not actually seen the accident but had seen its aftermath. Later we learn that he might not have even been there for the aftermath and that he has had to do quite a bit of inventing to fill in the story's details. Still later, he realizes that he had not been anywhere close to the events and might not have even been alive when they occurred. The implication is that the narrator is the author and that he is fully under the spell of stories that have the power to create reality, not just shape it. May's telling of the African fertility tale thus carries more weight than folklore: it highlights the power of fiction to transport listeners or readers, to create something lasting out of experience with the crucial aid of the voices that transmit stories.

The next story in the collection, "The Songs of Reba Love Jackson," indicates how much Wideman embraces this principle. Its protagonist is outside the family tree and the "Begat Chart" at the front of the book, and much of it takes place outside Homewood, though the last "song" in the series is dedicated to Homewood and affirms how important the place was to the protagonist. Reba Jackson is a gospel singer, and the story tells her life's story in snippets, each of which is a song she performs. It is significant that she repeatedly connects songs with stories and denies that she is creating anything with her songs: "I just sang the old songs and let them take me where they wanted to go" (124). The life of the artist is not important except as a conduit for the old songs, or stories.

The remaining stories evoke the very personal—so much so that one, "Across the Wide Missouri," reads like a memoir, portending Wideman's longstanding inquiry into the blurred boundaries between fiction and true stories. The autobiographical voice that broke through in "Lizabeth: The Caterpillar Story" dominates this piece about John and his estranged father. It is a brief meditation on fathers, sons, and memory, a rehearsal for Wideman's 1994 memoir *Fatheralong*. This story is about loss, but the following stories about brothers (and brothers-in-law), "Rashad" and "Tommy," are even more charged with a sense of cultural decay. "Rashad" tells the story of its title character's pattern of addiction and abuse as he suffers from time spent in the Vietnam War. Its central symbol is a banner Rashad made when he was in Vietnam, depicting his daughter Keesha against a backdrop of a Vietnamese landscape. The likeness is not good, and although the banner hangs for years, the story is about the act of removing it from the wall, perhaps in an attempt to remove Rashad's sins from the family's memory. Lizabeth does not know what to do with the banner once she takes it down, but it unleashes in her an enraged desire to knock down all the chipped and cracked plaster walls around her. She considers how alike Rashad and her son Tommy are and channels her rage into prayer, but the prayer itself feels like her burden: "A long hard prayer and it will be like hoisting the red bricks of Homewood A.M.E. Zion on her shoulders and trying to lift the whole building or trying to lift all of Homewood" (154). As the matriarch she considers this her duty, but Lizabeth's weariness builds throughout the collection, making it seem unlikely that she will be able to sustain this role.

"Tommy" is the first time Wideman tells the story of his brother Robby, to whom the collection is dedicated. His story is told much more fully in *Hiding Place*, *Brothers and Keepers*, and later works. The theme of decay is signaled early on as Tommy considers his neighborhood "like somebody's mouth they let some jive dentist fuck with. All these old houses nothing but rotten teeth and these raggedy pits is where some been dug out or knocked out and ain't nothing left but stumps and snaggleteeth just waiting to go. Thinking, that's right. That's just what it is. Why it stinks around here and why ain't nothing but filth and germs and rot. And what that make me? What it make all these niggers?" (160). The suggestion is not that the neighborhood's decline causes Tommy's nihilistic crime spree but rather that the neighborhood and the people who inhabit it decline simultaneously. True to Robby's story, Tommy is involved in a botched robbery during which a man is murdered, and he ends his story on the lam, seeking refuge at John's house out west. John makes the connection between the parallel declines of his neighborhood and its inhabitants, and it pains him to look at his brother's face as a result: "Too many faces in his brother's face. Starting with their mother and going back and going sideways and all of Homewood there if he looked long enough. Not just faces but streets and stories and rooms and songs" (174). All the Homewood stories are attempts to suggest the general through the particular, and this moment is a distilled version of this tendency.

In "Solitary" the subjects are the decay of Homewood and its effect on Lizabeth in particular. After an emotionally harrowing visit to her incarcerated son (clearly Robby), Lizabeth returns to Homewood and wanders the streets, noticing changes, especially that "her men were gone, gone, gone" (184). Long the pillar of faith in her family, she experiences a crisis of belief and confesses it to her brother Carl. She claims to understand her own mother's loss of faith and weariness late in life. The final image is ambiguous as she sees a train hurtling down the tracks and compares it to her God. She had always been afraid of walking over the bridge because she wouldn't know whether to run or to jump under the wheels of the onrushing train: "She'd wait this time, hold her ground this time. She'd watch it grow larger and larger and not look away, not shut her ears or stop her heart" (189). It is unclear whether this moment signals the restoration of her faith, or renewed courage, or suicidal despair.

The concerns of the collection come together impressively in its final piece, "The Beginning of Homewood." The author muddles the definitions of stories and letters, as he did in the initial dedication to his brother Robby. Here he places the story of Tommy next to the story of Sybela Owens, their ancestor who escaped slavery, gave birth to twenty children, and founded both Homewood and the author's family. Her "crime" liberated her from slavery; Robby's led him into confinement. The comparison is a difficult one for the author to make, and it depends, as always, on the story going a little further. Three times in the final two pages he says that a given story "could end here" (204, 205), but it keeps going: "So the struggle doesn't ever end. Her story, your story, the connections"

(205). Sybela's story is rendered in the voice of Aunt May, the storyteller who is the model for Wideman's Homewood aesthetic. To preserve the stories and keep them going, which is his principle aim, Wideman must acknowledge the complexity of the stories and honor the past by juxtaposing it with the present. There may be a beginning to Homewood, but although there has been a noticeable decline, there is no end, at least not as long as stories continue to be told.

Hiding Place, published the same year as *Damballah,* can be seen as both an attempt to retell stories and an homage to the blues aesthetic in which the blues are personalized and varied, rather than fully invented, by the artist. The central plot line of *Hiding Place* is, again, Tommy's crime and his initial attempts to evade the law. One of the chapters in the novel is a version of the story "Tommy" in *Damballah,* some of the language identical. *Hiding Place* is built on the interspersed narratives of three characters: Tommy, his great-great-aunt Bess, and a lackey named Clement who runs errands from the local barbershop. Bess lives on Bruston Hill, above Homewood, where Sybela Owens first landed to establish the community and her family. Tommy climbs the hill to seek asylum in her house after getting caught up in the robbery that led to murder. The tension between Tommy and Bess—their separate perspectives in need of reconciliation—fuels the narrative. Clement is the bystander who is the only witness to their interaction. This triangular pattern of characters is one Wideman has relied on before (notably in *A Glance Away*) and will use in later novels such as *Two Cities* (1998).

Clement is the least developed of these three characters, but his perspective opens the book. He is described as "feebleminded" (15) by the men who sit idly around the barbershop and gossip. His role is to listen and to run errands. He is an intermediary character, one who connects Bess (whom he calls Miss Bess and others call Mother Bess) to the Homewood neighborhood from which she is alienated. Many believe that she possesses the magical powers of a witch, but Clement thinks that she silently calls him and that his interactions with her help give shape to his life. On the day the novel opens, he climbs Bruston Hill as he always does to bring her provisions from the store. He hears her interactions with Tommy, specifically her repeated, curt refusal ("No") to Tommy's plea that she hide him. He self-consciously approaches, believing that both Tommy and Bess can see and hear him while he eavesdrops on the porch. His saving grace is his fertile imagination: he thinks of Tommy as a ghost, he hears Bess calling to him when she needs him, and he sees himself as a superhero cruising around Homewood on roller skates to complete his errands. Because he is able to daydream, he is immune to the troubles of Homewood that isolate Bess, infect the soul of Tommy, and provide nothing more than gossip for the men in the barbershop.

Belief is at the heart of the novel. Bess only believes in the past—her memory as well as the stories she once heard. In her first section of the novel, she relives a memory that she calls a "story she is watching and hearing as somebody tells it, somebody not her because she doesn't believe anything anymore" (22). Her reputation for being a witch stems from her being isolated, elderly, and mean. Her initial rejection of Tommy bears this out, but her memories suggest another side of her. Bess's story is one of loss: she lost her religion, her son, and "her man" (referred to as such throughout the novel but identified as Riley Simpkins in the family tree). She lives in a house that is a symbol of loss, described as decrepit by the other members of her family, a shelter with no modern amenities and barely fit for humans. Yet it is a connection to the family's origins as Bess was a young girl playing in the yard when Sybela Owens rocked on the porch. Bess, through her own incessant rocking on the porch, wants to channel this familial past: "Maybe seeing what Mother Owens saw behind her blind eyes because when you rock long enough you start to look inside stead of outside" (29). Memories become her preferred reality and nostalgia her preferred mode of existence. She does not "believe in photographs" (31) because they freeze a moment in time, whereas memory is more supple and enables her to reanimate people. Yet she admits, "I been up here too long now. Too many new faces and I can't see nothing in them" (32). Tommy is one of these new faces, and their encounter represents a clash between her inability to attach any positive meaning to the present and his unwillingness to honor the past.

Tommy's initial problem is nihilism: he contemplates Pittsburgh from Bruston Hill and sees the vicious cycle that has trapped him: "The city was a circle and East Liberty niggers and Homewood niggers and West Hell niggers all the same, all dead and dying down there on the same jive-ass merry-go-round. All of them lost as him" (37). His deep-seated fear of death intensifies this perspective, and the fact that Mother Bess has pronounced his doomed fate—"You was born to die" (34)—has further alienated him from himself and forced him to believe that he is worthless, which is how the community has always viewed him. And yet he comes to Bruston Hill not only because it is a safer hiding place than Homewood Avenue but because it is "the place in the stories all my people come from" (39). He is not only seeking refuge but also his origins, which might give meaning to his life. Even though she has refused his request for asylum, he remains on the hill, seeking comfort from the place while the police tighten their dragnet. He flees no farther than Bess's shed.

When she discovers him, she drags him out, and the true standoff between them begins. The reader learns more about the woman most residents of Homewood have dismissed as mean and evil. Her only son, Eugene, died two days after the end of World War II when a Japanese sniper, unaware that the war was over, killed him. This incident is not the only premature death of a child in the extended family, but it essentially undoes Bess and makes her resentful of the term "Mother Bess," which many use. She bitterly turns from her role as mother and embraces her role as lover to her husband, who, twenty years her elder, was destined to leave her a widow. In particular she reminisces about the way he would comb her hair while whistling "the blues he said, not the low down dirty or the lost my woman and gone or the good morning or good night blues but hair brushing blues" (49). She tries to complicate the moment, assuming that the blues he whistles must be related to the loss of their son and the inability of their love to counterbalance that loss, "but he just said hair brushing blues and smiled at me and I let it be" (49). This is an important moment in terms of defining the blues as something personal, the meaning of which is neither simple nor easily explained.

Tommy's presence angers her because he is part of the new generation of men who are unlike her man in that they resist monogamy and do not provide for their children. On a deeper level, though, Tommy reminds her of the death of Shirley's baby (Tommy's niece Kaleesha), which of course reminds her of the death of her son: "That boy's feet belonged down the hill, down in the Homewood streets and that's where they should have stayed because now she couldn't help herself, couldn't stop making the connections she knew she'd have to make" (51). Kaleesha's funeral was the moment when Bess decided she would never leave Bruston Hill, so as to be alone with her thoughts without feeling judged by her younger family members. She has a vision of an angel during the service and yearns for the past, wishing for "old time music, old time preaching, the word not spoken but chanted" (54). Tommy is evidence of cultural decline, in her mind, because he does not appear moved by music during the service. He is flummoxed by her because he is unable to work any verbal magic on her, which he considers his only gift. He contemplates her house, which reminds him of a slave cabin, providing an unconscious link to the troubles of history. He remembers a tender moment with his wife, Sarah, before his substance abuse and crimes ruined the relationship. He calls this memory a story and angrily thinks that "stories are lies" (79) when the memory does not last. Tommy's ambivalence toward the past is part of what makes him a complex character: he asks that Bess tell him a story, and she tells him how his mother, Lizabeth, was born blue because she could not breathe and how the storyteller May ran the baby outside and planted her in a snowbank, thus saving her life. Tommy claims, "All that old time stuff don't make me no never mind. Wasn't even born yet" (82). Yet the story apparently intrigues him because he asks for more details. However, he is not grateful for her stories or for her tough-love lessons, and he fantasizes about violently dispatching her.

Their vexed relationship signals a family in crisis, a broad generation gap, and a neighborhood in decline, all stemming from Tommy's troubles and Bess's irrevocable sense of loss.

As the novel continues, these two alienated relatives grow closer. They talk over moonshine-laced coffee about their separate perspectives, and Tommy reveals the existence of his son, Clyde. In the bar Clement listens to a conversation between Tommy's uncle Carl and John, who has returned to town from Wyoming to help the family deal with Tommy's trouble. John admits of Tommy, "Sometimes I get close to hating him. . . . I think about all he's done, all the people he's hurt" (102). Although he does not believe that Tommy is totally to blame for the way he behaves, John is frustrated that Tommy does not seem to seek anything beyond self-gratification. Indeed, we learn that Tommy was high when Clyde was born. His drug use led to his first stint in jail, when Sarah stops bringing Clyde to visit him. He plays out his life in a series of dreams (memories) while in jail, noting the decline of Homewood but still feeling attached to the place. He compares the destruction of Homewood to the way he ruined Sarah's life, partly admitting guilt and partly indulging in self-pity as he comes to terms with his reputation for being "cold," "evil," and "good for nothing" (114). That he is someone whose efforts have failed and whose nihilism has been intensified (if not caused) by constant rejection is closer to the truth: Sarah treats him no differently from how Bess treats him, ordering him away when he is most in need. His fear of death makes it especially difficult for him to deal with Clyde: he wants to make light of death, but he is too anxious. Something within him yearns for freedom, something "so strong that it made him turn his back on Sarah and turn his back on his son, so strong it could split open his skin" (122). He struggles with these feelings and wonders what his legacy to his son will be. The pressures behind these revelations are what involved him in the botched robbery that led to murder.

The long section that reveals Tommy's past is important in terms of establishing pathos. Bess reveals a sympathetic part of her past that links her to Tommy: when Tommy's sister Shirl brought her infant, Kaleesha, to Bess, the old woman bonded with the child and recognized generations of her relatives in the child's face. When Kaleesha died, Bess was left with renewed feelings of survivor's guilt: "ain't nothing else to say when babies die and old dried-up just as soon dead as alive things like me left walking the earth. What kind of a world is that?" (132). She continues to dismiss and judge Tommy, but she now connects him with the loss and sorrow that has always been attached to family. She convinces him to help plant her garden, and the exchange between them about whether the seeds he plants are "dead" says much about their shared anxieties over family and death; she says of the seeds, "Course they dead. Supposed to be dead. Why else you think you bury em in the ground? They dead and you put em in the ground so they can die some more, so they can split open and come apart and get mixed up with what's in the soil and go to growing again" (146). Perhaps not fully understanding the metaphor, Tommy complains about how difficult gardening is, and Bess, with what seems like genuine affection for the first time, believes that he is capable of learning something from her. Eventually there is mutual respect and affection in their banter even as they seem aggressive toward one another. Tommy has stayed with Bess three days, and there is a sort of resurrection of his spirit. Bess admires his defiant will to live, but she remains concerned about one thing: "Youall missed the blues. . . . Youall ain't never heard no music" (150). She has witnessed suffering, and in the past music was there to help process it. Tommy, however, has only drugs and the open road. This difference remains a concern to her: without the blues or gospel, Tommy and his ilk are spiritually doomed. And yet he had been whistling the blues. He knows the music, but as with his relationship to past stories, he does not seem to value it. Her final response to him is maternal, though, as she becomes Mother Bess once again, a name she has rejected. As the police storm Bruston Hill to take Tommy into custody, Bess burns down her shack while reuniting with her man in her imagination, determined to tell everyone that Tommy is innocent of the crime of murder, that he deserves a second chance, and that "they better make sure it don't happen so easy ever again" (158). The "it" of the final phrase is ambiguous, but refers partially to the ruin of Tommy's life. The irony is that Bess, on the verge of death, will not be able to communicate her wisdom to anyone, at least not in a direct, literal way. Still, Bess's final gesture is triumphant because she has overcome the fear that has holed her up in her own "hiding place," and Wideman wants the reader to see it that way; speaking of the vision he had of the book's ending, he said, "I saw an old woman walking out of the burning house; not scared nor frightened."[9]

Sent for You Yesterday, the third installment of the Homewood Trilogy, demonstrates the maturing of Wideman's Homewood aesthetic. Alan Cheuse in the *New York Times* claimed that the novel, which won the PEN/Faulkner Award, was evidence that "Mr. Wideman has come into his full powers. He is a literary artist with whom any reader who admires ambitious fiction must sooner or later reckon."[10] The reader of the trilogy encounters many of the same characters, stories, and motifs from the other two works (with echoes from the early novels, especially *A Glance Away*). This repetition has a number of effects: the reader becomes more conscious of storytelling as a vehicle for transmitting culture, the stories have different meanings when placed in different contexts, there is a tendency to mythologize certain figures and incidents, and characters that might have seemed fictional upon first encounter become more and more real. To some extent, the reader joins the family. *Sent for You Yesterday* brings this point home by emphasizing the author's alter-ego, nicknamed "Doot" in this novel, who has returned all ears, ready to receive and transmit his family stories over and over again.

The novel is divided into three sections and again centers around three main figures: Brother Tate—an albino first introduced in *A Glance Away,* though not exactly the same character—his adoptive sister, Lucy, and her long-term lover, Carl (Doot's uncle, who is an important figure in *Hiding Place*). There are a number of other characters, as the novel spans much of the twentieth century—the legendary patriarch John French and his piano-playing rogue friend Albert Wilkes also figure prominently—but the complex relationship between Brother, Lucy, and Carl is the main focus here. The novel opens with Brother Tate in heaven, telling a story to a friend. The story is actually a dream, as many stories are in this novel, and the effect of Brother's dream about riding a train (a recurrent symbol in the novel) is to render him mute, which parallels what happened in reality: Brother does not speak for sixteen years after the death of his son Junebug. He explains it in terms of pure fear that cannot be translated. The auditor does not understand the dream and downplays its potency, but Brother insists that the paralysis it produces is what makes it real: "Couldn't scream. Had to hold it in for sixteen years. Fraid to open my mouth for sixteen years cause I knowed I'd hear that scream" (11). This prologue introduces a number of motifs that permeate the novel: the way dreams and stories can be interpreted differently, the fact that stories are weak ("a shitty-tailed nothing kind of dream" [10]) until they are given significance, the importance of fate, and the primacy of individual experience.

Paralleling the author's exile and return, the first section, "The Return of Albert Wilkes," chronicles the reappearance of a man who left Homewood, but Albert Wilkes is more like Tommy than John. Accused of shooting a white police officer, Albert is a kind of folk hero in the tradition of Staggerlee or Railroad Bill, more notorious than heroic. He is known for drinking and carousing but also for playing piano. He is a slippery figure even after his return: the community does not know exactly where he is, and tales about who saw him where and when become the stuff of legend. Freeda in particular is concerned because Albert's return will invariably lead to John French's disappearance as Albert will tempt John to shirk his familial duties.

The section does not begin directly with Albert's return, though, but with Brother. (Before the novel's publication, Wideman said in an interview that the "working title" of the novel was *Brother Hall,*[11] indicating the centrality of this character.) Initially the narrator describes his own relationship to Brother, who is a mysterious figure (like Clement in *Hiding Place*) whose appearance and constant scatting in place of talking render him unique and integral to the place: "His strange color and silence were part of Homewood, like the names of the streets and the night trains and hills. But it wasn't exactly color and wasn't exactly silence. If you looked closely Brother had no color" (15). The people of Homewood are defined partially by their race, so Brother is a destabilizing force, one who causes the narrator (whom Brother christens "Doot" after one of his scat sounds) to think about identity in terms that go deeper than skin color. Brother's story is essentially that of another Wideman character who loses his son prematurely, and Doot assumes that Brother's affection for him is linked to the death of Junebug: "I'm linked to Brother Tate by stories, by his memories of a dead son, by my own memories of a silent, scat-singing albino man who was my uncle's best friend" (17). This realization gives Doot the license to reanimate Brother in stories and to explore the nuances of his story and his interiority. Brother stopped speaking when Doot was five years old, but the story begins before Doot's birth, when Brother and Carl were teens trying to scare each other by running in front of trains, on the day when Albert Wilkes returned to Homewood.

The aesthetic Wideman advances in *Sent for You Yesterday* and develops throughout his career thereafter involves his ability to appear and disappear fluidly as a first-person narrator. In doing so, he is able to introduce themes that are a combination of stories and his interpretation of them. For instance, his conception of Cassina Way, where his grandparents, mother, uncles, and aunts lived, reinforces the novel's emphasis on movement and on the paradoxical nature of Homewood's ability to intensify the experience of living but also to take lives arbitrarily. The identity of each individual he describes is both unique and connected: "The life in Cassina Way was a world apart from Homewood and Homewood a world apart from Pittsburgh and Pittsburgh was the North, a world apart from the South, and all those people crowded in Cassina Way carried the seeds of these worlds inside their skins, black, brown and gold and ivory skin which was the first world setting them apart" (21). Race is only one factor that sets his characters apart; they become individuals through their unique experiences, which are mythologized through repeated storytelling.

For example, the caterpillar-shaped scar on Freeda French's hand, which she obtained when she smashed the window to save her husband from a gunman, recurs in this story, but it becomes the beginning of a lengthy meditation on Freeda's individual life. She is anxious that things (and people) will disappear in the instant she glances away. She is consumed by memories, but she does not believe they are what give her life its unique shape: "If her life had a shape, the shape was not what she could remember, but what kept tearing her away, the voice which could look and look away" (32–33). Identity is determined by one's unique perception, and it is the job of the novelist to ascertain an individual's perspective as a way of animating his or her character. Freeda ruminates about the ephemeral nature of a soap bubble on her hand, which leads the reader to understand why she wants to know where her husband is after Albert Wilkes returns to town. Her anxiety is reflected in the experiences of other characters, such as Brother's unwillingness to speak after the death of Junebug. Along with her anxiety is her subtle prejudice about the "people from the deep South [who] started arriving with their dirty boxes and bags and spitting in the street and throwing garbage where people have to walk" (35). She is light-skinned and considers herself above certain aspects of black folk culture that her husband embraces, such as indelicate talk and especially blues music. When John French brings a Victrola into their house, she becomes agitated and threatens to smash all his records, which prefigures one of the key incidents at the end of the novel. Her desperate attempts to find John after Albert returns can be seen as her futile desire to control him and prevent him from following the general dissolution of Homewood.

Like Freeda, Albert feels a sense of propriety about Homewood, and he believes that Homewood would disappear if it were not in his consciousness. He returns as he left, shrouded in mystery, carrying nothing. The town gossips argue over who first spotted Albert when he returned, but the narrative shifts into his consciousness, revealing that he, like Freeda, is aware of the changes in Homewood. He had left Homewood just after playing the piano in the Tates' house, and he returns to that same piano, playing it again while Mrs. Tate tells stories of the past. While doing so he remembers a dream about a piano that is also a hurtling train, recalling Brother's dream from the prologue. Trains and pianos represent both life/movement and death/stasis. The Tates' piano is where Albert leaves his legacy for Homewood residents just before he flees, but it is also where the police eventually shoot him in retribution for murdering the white police officer.

Some members of the community consider this murder self-defense since the officer intended to murder Albert, who had a reputation for sleeping with white women. Albert believes that the misery he and others in Homewood suffer is racially motivated, and he expresses this idea to John French, who is also sensitive to misery around him but does not subscribe to all of Albert's theories. His perspective comes from his youth, when he lived in poverty and was once told by his father that he did not deserve the world's finer things: "Your black head ain't made for no satin pillow" (71). The two men debate why John is a family man and Albert is not, which is really a debate about character. John is regarded as a little wild but not necessarily bad, while Albert is considered trouble. Yet his version of trouble might be why he is a folk hero: he is not afraid to carry on affairs with white women, to come and go as he pleases, and to play the piano like no one else can. His effect is profound on John French and on the other men who hang around the Bucket of Blood bar in Homewood: Albert is a ghostly presence when he is not around. When he returns, John regards him as a yardstick to measure the changes that he himself cannot fully articulate because he does has no distance from them. Attracted to Albert's freedom, John angrily stalks away from a potential job, compromising his status as a family man. The two talk over a jug of wine, measuring how different they really are. Albert seems keen to lure John out of his family-man ways and reminds him that he was not always faithful to Freeda: in fact, the missing piece of the story about Freeda smashing the window to save John is that the man sneaking up to shoot John was seeking revenge for John's philandering. As if to drive home this point, the section ends with Freeda questioning John's commitment to his family, telling him that the worry she experienced that day was the only real trouble in the world. John reveals that Albert is hiding at the Tates' house with Brother and Lucy, who are children at this point, and Freeda correctly predicts that there is no refuge for Albert: the police will find him. The situation recalls Tommy's situation in *Hiding Place,* and the recurrent lesson is that trouble will visit the children of Homewood despite the parents' efforts to prevent it.

The second section, "The Courting of Lucy Tate," chronicles Carl's early sexual encounters with Lucy, which lead to their lifelong relationship. This section takes place in 1941, six months after Doot's birth. Brother remains a central figure even as the focus shifts to the other two members of "the three musketeers," as they call themselves. Brother proves to be a prodigy at the piano when he is twenty-one. When he plays at the Elks one night, patrons connect his abilities to Albert Wilkes, who has been dead seven years, but Carl sees the connection as more mystical than literal, as Brother would not have been able to learn from Albert when he was a young boy. Brother stops playing piano at the same time he stops talking, abandoning these forms of communication in favor of scatting, which is a hybrid alternative, fitting for an in-between figure such as Brother.

Albert's ghost inhabits the Tates' house and frightens the adolescent Carl, but he is still drawn to Lucy. During their first sexual encounter, she grotesquely produces a fragment of Albert's skull before they make love, recounting the story of how Albert had met his violent end while playing piano in their parlor (echoing Orion's severed head in "Damballah"). The experience ruined all music for her from that point on. She immediately retreats from Carl, sending a hostile note suggesting that she is in control of the relationship. Brother delivers the letter, and thus Carl believes that "Brother was part of it. Would always be. The three of them together in it now. Whatever *it* was" (110). Carl and Lucy only make love two more times over the following ten years. Their second encounter is again tinged by violence as Carl has cut himself while mowing, and Lucy takes on the role of nurse. The next time they make love is after he has been in the army, focused again on death, the "stacks of dead Japanese marines" (115) that he has to bulldoze over a cliff, as well as his dead comrades whom he has to carry on his back.

Doot reintroduces himself into the story at this point, reiterating the way he constructs these stories from a combination of memory and the repetition of the stories he has heard. He has returned to Homewood at the age of thirty to hear them again from the mouths of Lucy and Carl themselves, who talk with the teasing impatience of a couple who has been together a long time. Doot compares the stories he has heard to his grandfather's hat, which he still keeps: "Timeless, intimidating, fragile" (117). He has come back to hear more about Brother, but he remains impatient with the rhythms of Uncle Carl's storytelling (interspersed with Lucy's comments). Carl says, "You listening but you ain't hearing, Doot" (121). Doot does not understand the unique nature of Brother, the way he could communicate without talking. The story turns to Junebug's death, which involves not Lucy's courtship as the title implies, but Brother's courtship of Samantha (Sam). The story unfolds like a handheld fan, and it happens in Lucy's mind rather than as an exchange between Carl and Lucy without "her helping words, her amens, her reminders of dates, of names" (124). This is more evidence that Wideman is conscious of the nature of storytelling and its relationship to his fiction: it is dependent on voices, sometimes in concert with one another and sometimes in isolation.

The story of Junebug moves back and forth across time according to the movements of Lucy's memory. It involves taking baths with Brother when she was young, Brother's death, and visiting Sam in a mental institution before it gets to their relationship and the birth and death of Junebug. Sam is as eccentric a figure as Brother, as black as he is white, and disdainful of white people, though intrigued by Brother because of his unusual combination of white skin and black features. Her mission is to raise as many black children as she can bear in what she calls "the Ark," her safe home within Homewood that will eventually lead to a Promised Land. Her ideology interferes with her relationship with Brother even as they make love. Even after researching albinism at the library, she continues to associate blackness with royalty and assumes that Brother's lack of pigment is a threat to blackness. When Junebug is born with albinism, Sam's eight other children immediately react to their sibling's difference, and even Sam admits that she "blamed little Junebug and cursed his white skin and his ghost daddy cause I had to make a choice" (138) between loving Junebug and loving the other children. When Junebug dies in a fire,

Sam is confused between what she calls "the facts"—that the child died by accident—and her "dream" that his siblings caused the fire. Dreams become her reality, and they are reminiscent of Brother's dream, which opens the prologue, in that she is paralyzed and ridden with guilt. The tale links empathy with storytelling: Sam has to inhabit Junebug's consciousness to come to terms with the possibility that he was killed by her other children, and Lucy similarly has to inhabit Sam's consciousness: "If you tell Junebug's story you have to be Samantha" (145). The next layer is that Doot has to become Lucy to tell all of these stories. He also has to have the right perspective, as Uncle Carl tells him: "People ain't easy to see. . . . Get closer and closer and things come apart and the tiniest bit of anything is big as the world" (148). This describes the unfolding of Wideman's stories: details that seem insignificant become magnified and examined from multiple angles until they are redolent with meaning. The section ends with Carl talking about the way he, Brother, and Lucy all became addicted to dope, then became clean again. Doot had ostensibly wanted to hear about Brother, but Carl says, "how Ima tell his [story] without telling mine. And Lucy's" (154). This is another dimension of stories in the Homewood trilogy: they are all intertwined.

The third section of the book, "Brother," retells Brother's story over time in a series of four dated vignettes spanning from 1941 to 1970, which is when Doot has returned to listen to Carl's and Lucy's stories. The first vignette is a dream that unifies many of the novel's symbols and motifs: trains, the death of Albert Wilkes, and the necessity of inhabiting another person's being in order to understand fully their experiences. Brother becomes Albert in the dream, then he is both Albert and Brother, and then he is fully Brother and identified as the person who tells the police that Albert is in the Tates' house, causing them to burst in and murder him at the piano. He is unsure when he wakes up what is true memory and what is a product of his invented dream-mind. It is the first time he has had the train dream, and the dream returns in the second vignette, which takes place in 1946, the year of Junebug's death. It is largely an internal monologue about Junebug's death, especially about how Brother built the infant a coffin and stayed with him on the night he died. In this moving, lyrical section, he affirms something like faith and connects to both his progeny and his ancestry on a deep level: "*I been through it before. . . . It all starts up again in you. It's all there again. You are in me and I am in you so it never stops*" (171). The novel's epigraph begins, "Past lives live in us, through us." Wideman's relationship to past lives, including Brother's and even little Junebug's, is clear from these statements. Brother suffers a crisis of conscience, wondering if he had "lied to his son" (171) about the afterlife and reincarnation, but he also is able to conceive of his own soul detached from his body. This is the moment when he elects to stop speaking: “he had said enough and wouldn’t say any more” (172).

The third vignette, on the night of Brother’s death in 1962, continues his inquiry into faith as he attends a revival meeting and follows its procession through Homewood. He recalls his vision of his soul departing from his body and moves toward the train tracks, where he lays his head down. There had been speculation throughout the novel about whether Brother killed himself or not, and this vignette leaves it ambiguous. In Brother’s mind his final gesture is a renewal of the “scare game” he and Carl had played when they were young, and he is demonstrating to his dead son, Junebug, that he is not scared, that fear can be overcome. In the final section Lucy returns from the bar and waits for Doot and Carl to return, bumping into the ghosts of her memories. She recalls a paper bag full of drawings: Carl’s from art school on one side of each sheet and Brother’s on the other side. All of Brother’s figures have wings on them, emphasizing his spiritual quest or his angelic role in the lives of others. He also renders the people of Homewood in their younger days, just as Wideman does in his fiction: art conquers aging and death. When Doot and Carl return, the three of them talk about the effect of revisiting the old stories. The conversation causes Lucy to think of the “How Long Blues,” which begins, “I can hear the whistle blowing / Can’t see the train” (196). It is an homage to the “old Homewood people” who taught Lucy “you don’t have to give up” (198). This group includes Brother, and Lucy argues, “They were special people. Real people. Took up space and didn’t change just because white folks wanted them different” (199). There is a dignity to Brother’s story despite his suffering and apparent lack of conventional success. Like that of John French and Albert Wilkes, his heroism was in his adherence to his individual will. Lucy tells Doot a story from his youth, of the first time he danced. Her memory confuses a number of events from over the years, and she wonders what happened to all the blues records they used to listen to, John French’s collection, which helped bring the family together and unite them with a larger tradition. While she does not tell Doot, she privately remembers how, during her junkie period, a doped-up acquaintance named Rodney Jones smashed the records, and the memory of it brings her to tears. But the three of them push beyond the sadness of loss and reconnect through music as the ghosts of Albert Wilkes and Brother appear to join the party.

The Homewood Trilogy chronicles much suffering, violence, and untimely death. Balancing those forces is a celebration of characters who survive and whose spirits are defiant. They are connected as family and through storytelling. Moreover, the deteriorating neighborhood of Homewood is resurrected rather than condemned in the trilogy; as Guzzio notes, "Wideman names and re-names Homewood, not as a ghetto, but as a site of heritage and history that is intimately connected with his own family."[12] Wideman deliberately attempted to blend fiction, mythology, and nonfiction in these works; and they prepared him for more forays into nonfiction proper, which would provide him with the opportunity to retell the truth in new ways and continue to develop his unique style, liberated from the conventions of any one genre.

CHAPTER 4

Brothers and Fathers

The Homewood Trilogy was a stylistic breakthrough for Wideman that earned him notoriety and critical respect. Although he would continue to revisit Homewood and its inhabitants in subsequent works, he would find different ways to approach it. One change the Homewood Trilogy brought about was Wideman's willingness to experiment with genre. These works of fiction had strong biographical and autobiographical elements. His memoirs *Brothers and Keepers* and *Fatheralong* might be described as biography and autobiography with strong fictional elements. As Guzzio wrote, "Trying to decide what is fiction and what is nonfiction in his work is like wading through quicksand and, ultimately, misses the goal of Wideman's aesthetic."[1] This is true of much of his work, which straddles the line between fiction and nonfiction, but these two books—among his most celebrated and enduring—are perhaps the only two that can be classified as pure nonfiction. Together they showcase Wideman's concerns with self and family but also use those topics to explore a number of related social issues, including incarceration, racial identity, and history.

Ishmael Reed's review of *Brothers and Keepers* in the *New York Times* was positive, even as close to gushing as Reed gets. He opened the review by describing it as "gripping" and "a rare triumph in its use of diverse linguistic styles," and concluded, "Mr. Wideman has succeeded brilliantly in both understanding his brother's life and coming to terms with his own."[2] The hybrid of biography and autobiography Reed alluded to is what gives the book much of its power, and critics have held it up as a model of life writing. *Brothers and Keepers* retells the story of his brother Robby, first chronicled in the Homewood Trilogy, but the form (nonfiction) and the perspective (Wideman's own mixed with Robby's) combine to produce a work of unique poignancy. The basic conundrum Wideman faces is to figure out why he and his brother ended up on such separate paths: one an award-winning novelist, Rhodes Scholar, and professor, the other incarcerated for life for his involvement in a robbery and murder. Wideman exposes the difficulty of this conundrum repeatedly. In a single paragraph he writes, "Even the voice, the words he chose were mine in a way. We're so alike, I kept thinking," followed by the opposite point of view: "He was the criminal. I was the visitor from outside. Different as night and day" (76). Wideman's deep interpretation of a layered reality prevents him from coming to facile conclusions about why he and his brother play such different roles.

As Eugene Philip Page argued, one possible interpretation for this disparity is related to the differences in Wideman's parents—his tireless, faithful mother and his emotionally distant father—altered and replayed in his relationship with Robby.[3] In this sense *Brothers and Keepers* continues Wideman's genealogical project evident in the Homewood novels. In one stunning passage he conceives of an alternative to the familiar figure of the family tree, replacing it with an inverse pyramid that balances on top of the self: "Everybody needs one father, two grandfathers, four great-grandfathers, eight great-great-grandfathers, sixteen great-great-great-grandfathers, then thirty-two, then sixty-four, and that's only eight generations backward in time, eight generations linked directly, intimately with what you are" (23–24). The vast range of traits represented by this enormous sampling of ancestry yields a mind-boggling number of combinations that might explain individual differences between him and his brother: "Think of a pyramid balanced on one of its points, a vast cone of light whose sides flare outward, vectors of force like the slanted lines kids draw to show a star's shining" (24). The figure is awe inspiring, but it could also be seen as a weight on Wideman's back: the weight of history and of family simultaneously. The title of the book alludes to the passage in the Bible in which Cain responds to God with a rhetorical question—"Am I my brother's keeper?"—feigning ignorance after having murdered Abel. Family can be a burden as well as a bond.

The weight of the pyramid is parallel to the weight of his brother's story, one Wideman has attempted to unload in fiction before, in a story in *Damballah* and over the course of *Hiding Place*. *Brothers and Keepers* gets at the question of connection even more directly. As Wideman said in the interview with Kay Bonetti regarding his many attempts to tell Robby's story, "I've been asking myself questions that have to do with how people are connected and what's at stake in these connections."[4] In *Hiding Place* the fictional John had said of his brother, ""Sometimes I get close to hating him. . . . I think about all he's done, all the people he's hurt" (102). While this judgment and condemnation are certainly understandable, Wideman strives to move beyond them, and *Brothers and*

Keepers is the record of that attempt. Its implications are much broader than the relationship between two brothers, for Robby represents a common stereotype: the black, urban criminal who is easily labeled and dismissed in the contemporary United States once he has been locked up for life. Wideman proves that all encounters between people invite deep conversations about self and other if we are willing to engage with them. In this work, Wideman forces himself beyond that early judgment to allow the reader to contemplate the ethical questions of incarceration as a remedy to social ills. We know what Robby did and can choose to end the story there. But Wideman elects to *begin* the story there, and *Brothers and Keepers* questions the origin point and end point of any story. Since Wideman has become adept at disrupting traditional plot structures, he is in a unique position to reconstruct Robby's story in a powerful way, and his commitment to listening to the people of Homewood pushes him to do so in Robby's own voice.

The title of the first section of the book, "Visits," denotes both Robby's visit to John while on the lam and John's visits to Robby in prison. Like his fictional alter-ego Tommy in *Hiding Place,* Robby is running at the beginning of *Brothers and Keepers,* and in the final paragraph he indicates that he still has not fully told that part of his story or even really begun: "Mize well get back to the running, man. Mize well start telling you about it" (238). In the interview with Bonetti, Wideman admitted that his exile in Wyoming, "another semi-conscious break" from his life in Homewood, was also a form of running: "There was never a stage in my life when I was not very worried about both the direction in which I was running and what I was running from. . . . I was always somebody who had ghosts, who had demons. The hellhound was on my trail."[5] It is safe to assume that all of Wideman's early accomplishments—his Ivy League education, Rhodes scholarship, basketball triumphs, and successes as a fiction writer—were variations on this running, getting out of the limited and limiting possibilities of Homewood. Race complicates the direction of this running, as he discusses in *Brothers and Keepers:* his wife is white, the University of Pennsylvania was overwhelmingly white, and the population of Wyoming is among the whitest in the nation. The flight he has chosen has left him racially alienated to some degree. He states this idea explicitly: "I was running away from Pittsburgh, from poverty, from blackness" (26–27). Robby's return forces John to confront his divided self: "Easier to change the way I talked and walked, easier to be two people than to expose in either world the awkward mix of school or home I'd become" (27). In a 1995 interview he worried that he might have "oversold the idea of running away. I don't think I ever ran away from the black world in a kind of blind acceptance of something else. I made too much of a dichotomy between the white world and the black world. . . . It's too simple."[6]

The "visit" from Robby is in truth a moment of violent encounter: John's encounter with the past he had fled, with a version of his younger self he thought he had left behind. Repeatedly in interviews he has stated that he does not revisit works he has published. This "don't look back" mentality is something he had to overcome to change the trajectory of his aesthetic during the Homewood books. There is shame and guilt attached to his decision to leave Homewood and also fear and vulnerability. Referring to the fact that the Laramie police had identified four suspects in conjunction with Robby's crime, John says, "I was black. My brother was a suspect. So perhaps I was the fourth perpetrator. No matter that I lived four hundred miles from the scene of the crime. No matter that I wrote books and taught literature and creative writing at the university. I was black. Robby was my brother. Those unalterable facts would always incriminate me" (14). He is alluding to racial profiling on the part of the police here, but there is also a deeper psychological element involved with the fact that Robby is his brother, a bond that implicates him no matter how much he resists it: "Robby was inside me. Wherever he was, running for his life, he carried part of me with him" (4). They had been labeled and defined against one another from youth—the good seed and the bad seed, the student and the party boy—and these labels helped dictate their fates. But John acknowledges that he had a role in constructing their identities and, in doing so, he replicated the structure of the prison: "The problem was that in order to be the person I thought I wanted to be, I believed I had to seal myself off from you, construct a wall between us" (26). He extends the metaphor, suggesting that he has been the one in prison: "I continued to feel caged by my bewilderment, by my inability to see clearly, accurately, not only the last visit with my brother, but the whole long skein of our lives together and apart. So this book. This attempt to break out, to knock down the walls" (18). It is significant that John is the one who is attempting to "break out" here. He recognizes the truth of his self-fashioning: "I'd adopted the strategy of slaves, the oppressed, the powerless. I thought I was running but I was fashioning a cage" (32).

"Visits" is a template for Wideman's later nonfiction in the way it gathers up virtually everything on his mind and lays it on the table for examination. At the heart of his musings about history, Homewood, and his brother's fate is a strong tendency toward confession. He feels both shame and anger when a pompous white student at Penn tells him, essentially, that he knows nothing about authentic blues music. He regards his beloved Homewood as a "briar patch" that is "always snatching [him] back" (39). He insinuates that he has been unfaithful in his marriage. All of this confession makes him quite anxious, and rather than dismissing his brother as one of the "bad guys," he finds himself staring into the uncomfortable abyss of the self and feeling displeased with what he finds: "I have a lot to hide. Places inside myself where truth hurts, where incriminating secrets are hidden, places I avoid or deny most of the time. Pulling one piece of that debris to the surface, airing it in the light of day doesn't accomplish much, doesn't clarify the rest of what's buried down there. What I feel when I delve deeply into myself is chaos. Chaos and contradiction" (97). This statement is partly self-recrimination, but it functions in the book to destabilize the notion that those labeled criminals are pure evil while those who are not are pure good. It is a way to begin to tell Robby's story with empathy rather than pity in mind.

To succeed at this project, John must sort out the proper process of constructing this book, which he does in a self-conscious way, talking about its origins, its fits and starts, its failures as well as its final shape. Writing it forces him to change the very role of the writer as he has come to understand it: "The hardest habit to break, since it was the habit of a lifetime, would be listening to myself listen to him. . . . Start fresh, clear the pipes, resist too facile an identification, tame the urge to take off with Robby's story and make it my own" (77). He thus begins the story in his own voice, really his own story, because he is anxious about the silence that ensues when he first encounters Robby in prison: "His own story freeing me, because it forces me to tell my own" (98). Yet he realizes this is only a way to begin: the story to be told is truly Robby's, and his own voice has the ability to interrupt or even push Robby's aside completely. He speaks of the awkwardness of their initial meetings and cautions himself against doing exactly what he does in the first section of the book: "Another book could be constructed about a writer who goes to a prison to interview his brother but comes away with his own story. The conversations with his brother would provide a stage for dramatizing the writer's tortured relationship to other people, himself, his craft. The writer's motives, the issue of exploitation, the inevitable conflict between his role as detached observer and his responsibility as a brother would be at the center of such a book" (78). These concerns are not "at the center" of *Brothers and Keepers,* either thematically or physically, but they certainly frame it. John has to force himself to listen, and at one point to actually put down his pen while listening to his brother, trusting that he will eventually discover the ability to transform his brother's told story into print.

The key to doing so is to render Robby's story in Robby's authentic voice. The second section of the book—"Our Time," the longest section—largely sets aside John's voice, his story, and his anxious concerns about the ethics of the whole project. Like the author, the reader is encouraged to listen. John's rendering the story in Robby's vernacular idiom facilitates this process. The fact of Robby's crime, which leaves one man dead, is incontrovertible, but the events leading to it are more complex as they attach themselves to a real man with a distinctive voice rather than to a concept (that is, Robby versus a "common criminal"). Wideman's project often involves exploring the specific as a way of getting at a general truth; in the interview with Bonetti, he said, "You have to be aware of the particular. You have to be aware of the specific people, the specific words, the specific locales and then something grows out of that."[7]

Once John has exposed something of his own story and learned to listen to Robby's, the book has two main remaining tasks: (1) to humanize Robby, not to present him as a victim but to link his individual study to a larger human struggle, and (2) to consider the validity of the treatment Robby and many other young black men endure in the contemporary American prison. Although Robby's voice is about to take over, this section of the book begins with John's rejection of conventional plots: "You never know exactly when something begins. The more you delve and backtrack and think, the more clear it becomes that nothing has a discrete, independent history; people and events take shape not in orderly, chronological sequence but in relation to other forces and events, tangled skeins of necessity and interdependence and chance that after all could have produced only one result: what is" (19). Backtracking is especially important here: the nonlinear rendering of Robby's tale is consistent with Wideman's novels, which consciously violate traditional plot structures to achieve their unique effects.

Brothers and Keepers suggests a number of places where Robby's story might "begin": the factors that led to the crime and punishment that constitute the harsh "what is" realities of his life in prison. One of the factors that pulled Robby into his lifestyle was the lure of ghetto stardom: he and his friends defined themselves against the "square" life that John and his other siblings chose, partly because that life had a very palpable (if illusory) version of glamour, partly because it trapped him early ("having lived in the 'life,' it becomes very hard—almost impossible—to find any contentment in joining the status quo" [57]), partly because he came of age during a period of black militancy that redefined success ("to be in was to be out—out of touch with the square world and all of its rules on what's right and wrong" [58]), and partly because there seemed to be no other options. Robby and John elect to begin the story not with Robby but with his friend Garth, who died young of a liver disease. Robby envisions himself and his friends as the fingers on a hand, each different, with Garth, the "dreamer" of the group, as the thumb. When Garth dies young, Robby despairs: "When you thought about it, Garth's dying made no sense. And the more you thought the more you dug that nothing else did neither. The world's a stone bitch" (64). This observation may not be the direct route to Robby's crime, but it is at least one source of his nihilism. He and his friends develop a sense of fatalism following the funeral, imagining that the white world had no sympathy for Garth's death: "Nigger wasn't going nowhere, nohow. . . . Wind up killing some innocent person or wasting another nigger" (64). They feel invisible and insubstantial, like the nameless boys in Ellison's *Invisible Man:* "Which one of the shadows in this black room would go first? What did it matter? Who cared? Who would remember their names; they were ghosts already. Dead as Garth already" (65). Robby's final frustration is that he is unable to come up with a fitting tribute to memorialize his fallen friend, and he lapses into silent anger as he and his surviving friends drift off in separate directions.

John backtracks from this version of the story to recall the first time he heard about Garth. It was from his mother, in 1975, just before Robby's arrest, six years before John started writing about it. Recalling his mother's version of the story, he realizes, "The story contained all the clues I'm trying to decipher now" (76). It is at this moment he realizes, "I'd lost my Homewood ear. Missed all the things unsaid that invested her words with special urgency" (76). He does not hear the panic in her voice, just the resignation that Robby was with a bad crowd, that he always seemed to be looking for trouble. Although she is worried about Robby and the influence of his friends on his fate, she also says, "I can't blame them. No jobs, no money in their pockets. How they supposed to feel like men?" (68). One of the effects of growing up in Homewood is the inevitability of attempting to switch one's perspective: "You tried on the other person's point of view. You sought the other, better person in yourself who might talk you into relinquishing for a moment your selfish interest in whatever was at issue" (69). Through including her story, John attempts to overcome his own selfish motivations. His initial tendency to see Robby as doomed and to hate him for victimizing their mother is too simple. It is not just his Homewood ear that he has lost but also the deep connection that it provides. This is not to say that everyone from Homewood thinks alike or believes the same things, only that there are shared connections among those who have lived there. A central concept in Wideman is to overcome the binary way of thinking that turns others into pariahs so that selves can be heroes. His mother's generous interpretation of Garth's story and Robby's response to it are key components in this realization. And yet John realizes that he and his brother are not interchangeable. There is still a fundamental difference between them, and it is caught up with his status as a writer. He wonders whether writing is a form of exploitation (77), a sentiment he repeats in later works such as *Fatheralong* and *The Island: Martinique.*

His solution to the conundrum he has identified—the connections between himself and his brother versus their essential differences—is to write *Brothers and Keepers* in two voices. For the remainder of the central section of the book,

Robby's own distinctive voice takes over, identifying a number of other possible starting points for his troubles: his realization of the realities of segregated neighborhoods, his desire as the youngest to rebel against his older siblings' versions of success, and the fact that his birthday was associated with multiple tragedies in Wideman family history. Robby leads the reader through his disintegration, from missing his own birthday party because he was strung out on drugs, to stealing a television from John to support his habit, and eventually to the fateful day of the crime that garnered him a life sentence. The first time he is arrested for drug possession he makes a pathetic suicide attempt in his cell, reiterating the feeling of worthlessness he first realized after Garth's death. John ruefully realizes that the first course he taught on black literature at Penn, especially the section on the Black Arts Movement, was all about his brother's life, but "I never even spoke to Robby. Never knew until years later that he was the one who could have told me much of what I needed to hear" (111).

But the more hopeful side of Robby's disintegration is his attempt to fashion himself into a hero of the revolution. One pivotal moment he recalls is a standoff with his father, a misguided one in which he menaces the elder man with a pair of scissors, but it taps into a sense that his rebellion at least has the potential to lead to empowerment. This moment flows into an extended period of fighting the police, when Robby describes himself as a "stone mad militant" (114), whose path to identity involves resistance to authority. The culmination of this period is his involvement in a strike at his high school based on demands for improved conditions and a black history course. He is proud of his oratorical skills and organizes a party in a nearby park following the successful strike. His exuberance ends quickly, though, when the authorities crack down following the strike, forcing Robby and his classmates to realize in no uncertain terms who runs the school. This is another pivotal setback for Robby, putting him on a course where drugs and crime seem the only options: "I knew I was doing wrong. Knew I was hurting people. But then I'd look around and see Homewood and see what was going down. Shit. I ain't gon lay down and die" (132). The reader may not be willing to forgive Robby for his crimes, but the fact that his story is rendered honestly, in his own voice, provides a context that would not otherwise be available.

In addition to providing the story of a marginalized individual, *Brothers and Keepers* also comments on the ethics of incarceration, particularly as it relates to other social structures that reinforce the power dynamics between black and white Americans. Robby sees his own neighborhood as one that was virtually manufactured to prevent the success of black men: "They crawling. They stepped on. Mize well be roaches or some goddamn waterbugs. White man got em backed up in Homewood and he's sprinkling roach powder on em" (152).

In prison he again feels powerless, and when the courts deny his appeal for a reduced sentence, his feelings of worthlessness are renewed. As a visitor, John shares these feelings. The condescending way he, his mother, and his children are treated when they visit Robby stirs up buried feelings he has not frequently confronted: "The black rage that makes you want to strike out and smash somebody's face because you know they have you by the throat, killing you by inches. You know you're being singled out, discriminated against simply because the person doing it to you has the power to get away with it and you're powerless to stop him" (187). Through a series of meditations on the nature of prisons, he begins to share some of Robby's despair, but through the writing of *Brothers and Keepers,* he arrives at a different, more hopeful conclusion. Robby's spirit is indomitable. Within prison he continues to change and grow. This appraisal arrives only once John discards his own artificial attempts "to impose a dramatic shape on a relationship" and instead to attend to "the inner changes, his slow, internal adjustment day by day to an unbearable situation" (194, 195). Through his attempts at education, his renaming himself Faruq while not fully buying into the ideology of the Nation of Islam, and even an improbable attempt to forge a romantic relationship with a woman on the outside, Robby becomes a hero in John's eyes rather than a victim: "Prison had changed my brother, not broken him, and therein lay the story" (195). Robby's ability to adapt and to some degree thrive in his miserable circumstances is paradoxically intertwined with the same personality traits that landed him in jail in the first place. John concludes, "I'm glad to see Robby's best (worst) parts have survived. Can't have one without the other" (198). Indirectly he is commenting on their relationship. He admits, "I had learned to shut my brother out of my mind. I could deal with his plight only by brutal compartmentalization" (221). This book records his attempts to unlearn that behavior, and to arrive at a way of thinking that does not depend on binary opposition.

In the postscript to *Brothers and Keepers,* John reveals that Robby's son Omar has started to visit him in prison and that this vital connection is "good news" because it brings father and son together despite negative circumstances. The father-son bond is one that Wideman explores in much greater detail in his next memoir, *Fatheralong.* The subtitle of this book only begins to glimpse its complexity: "A Meditation on Fathers and Sons, Race and Society." Its many subjects also foreground history and geography, and the meditation ranges from confession to sophisticated critical analysis. Stylistically, *Brothers and Keepers* showcases Wideman's fiction-writing skills to a greater degree, as its major accomplishment is the accurate representation of Robby's voice. *Fatheralong,* by contrast, shows Wideman becoming more comfortable with his own perspective in nonfiction. The precedent for Wideman's evolving nonfiction style is James Baldwin, particularly in his longer, expansive works like *The Fire Next Time, No Name in the Street,* and *The Devil Finds Work.*

Critical responses to *Fatheralong* have been nearly as laudatory as those to *Brothers and Keepers.* Jacqueline Berben-Masi, in a special issue of *Callaloo* on the European reception to Wideman, praised its many layers, saying "*Fatheralong* accommodates many moods, modes, and styles. It combines sequences of provocation, self-searching, healing, and acceptance; it rallies support through the direct address to the reader who is apostrophized at every turn; it sounds a call to arms to unify the disparate readership into a militant corps."[8]

Although the titles of both memoirs suggest that masculine identity is of primary importance, Wideman's mother and grandmother are very much in the spotlight in both. In *Brothers and Keepers* it is his mother who visits Robby in prison most frequently and who keeps the family together despite adversity. Robby speaks of how his behavior has affected her in particular. Fathers and husbands throughout Wideman's oeuvre are often described in terms of their absence or of their departures and returns. This pattern, established in the first two novels as well as the Homewood Trilogy, is borne out in these two memoirs.

Fatheralong contains some of Wideman's frankest statements about race, racism, and racial identity. In the opening section, "Common Ground," he speaks of what happens when two black people meet on the street, registering their unconscious connection regarding "the miracle and disgrace of our history" (ix). Black people are constantly engaged in nothing less than the definition of reality, more specifically "the work of giving meaning to difference" (x). Out of this shared condition comes individual identity: "Being *me,* not what difference makes of me" (xi). Wideman realizes he is stepping into quicksand by even attempting to discuss relationships and common identity in terms of race. Given the differences he explored in *Brothers and Keepers* between himself and his brother, neither race nor region nor even family is enough to explain why two individuals are who they are, and yet that book is an attempt to discover and identify vital connections despite the obvious differences between the author and his brother. In this opening essay, he acknowledges race as a common bond, yet he is immediately wary of it. The African continent is vast, history is too long, and genetic combinations produce too much variety: "Chaos looms because race can mean everything or nothing. A denial of diversity. A claim of profound, unalterable difference between kinds of human beings" (xii).

"Race" itself becomes not a category in Wideman's analysis but rather a weapon that could be used for subjugation or even genocide. The concept of difference automatically engenders inferiority, and while the definers of racial difference (historically Europeans) assert their own superiority based on race, "the oppressed, to the degree they internalized the message of race, became active agents of their oppression" (xiii). He uses this concept to interrogate specific patterns in history that might allow the oppressed to achieve some level of comfort in a world defined by racial difference (such as passing, integration, or the acknowledgment of the effects of miscegenation). He speaks not in terms of the African diaspora but of "the long European diaspora," during which the oppressors carried their concept of race to every corner of the globe: "The word *race* evokes a paradigm, a systematic network or pattern of assumptions, relationships, a model of reality, a history and causation as complete, closed, and pervasive as a religion. Race is not a set of qualities inhering in some 'other,' it's the license to ascribe such qualities allied with the power to make them stick" (xv). The concept of race is about power, specifically the power of definition. Invoking race signals "a game only one player, the inventor of race, can win" (xvi). He goes on to disturb the dividing line between "race" and "racism." The former purports to be neutral, the latter something denigrated by most members of society, but they are two versions of the same concept in Wideman's eyes. "Race" is never neutral. To invoke race is to reinforce difference-based power dynamics, even if the user of the term does not realize it. Historically, he argues, whites have naively viewed themselves as raceless. As an example, Wideman evokes a Supreme Court ruling about whether or not college admissions should be race-blind. Filing lawsuits such as the *Bakke* decision perpetuates "the terms of a debate we can't win because the terms of the debate already contain an understanding, a presumption of winner and loser" (xxi). "Race" takes away the power of individuals to determine their own stories on their own terms. The concept of race can only limit; Wideman encourages his readers to understand how much is possible when we move beyond it: "many black people are on the move, beyond the power of race to pigeonhole and cage" (xxii). The key to such progress is the acknowledgment of the importance of connections to earlier generations. He compares the situation of contemporary black Americans to a second Middle Passage, after which alienated slaves in the New World had to reinvent themselves without the benefit of traditional cultural and familial traditions. To honor the achievements of the past, to celebrate "music, new forms of bonding, revival and reexamination of heroes" (xxiii), Wideman sees the importance of pushing beyond "the paradigm of race," which is "the antithesis of freedom" (xxiv). This deep meditation launches another paradigm that is the substance of the book, and Wideman states his purpose in writing these memoirs explicitly: "They are an attempt, among other things, to break out, displace, replace the paradigm of race. Teach me who I might be, who you might be—without it" (xxv).

He begins the first essay with an account of his parents' separation, which he explicitly compares to "segregation" (4). His parents are awkward and uncomfortable in any social situation in which they must appear in the same room. This circumstance spurs Wideman to think about the distance between any two people, even those with a shared history who had once been in love. His own relationship with his father is inadequate because their time together had always been too hasty, their encounters too superficial. The book chronicles a series of their travels together late in life, beginning with Edgar driving John to the Pittsburgh airport. John had been listening raptly to his mother's stories in her apartment, and Edgar's knock on the door interrupts the spell. On their drive to the airport, John revives an idea to visit South Carolina, where his grandfather had been born. When he was younger and still deeply mired in "the paradigm of race," John had rejected the possibility, envisioning the lynching of Emmett Till on one end of the racial spectrum and cotton-picking, watermelon-eating, "crusty black" (16) people who talked funny on the other. The more mature John is now ready for a meaningful trip to his familial origins, and he and his father plan to travel there together.

The occasion of picking his father up for the journey south (which actually occurs three years later) causes John to brood about the public housing where his father lives and the decay of black, urban, industrialized cities of the North more generally. It is a subject that has troubled him viscerally for a long time, but it now seems more immediate as he and his father reverse the Great Migration that brought so many African Americans (including his ancestors) north a century earlier. John digresses into analyses of the privatization of public housing and the geography of South Carolina as they make their way from Pittsburgh to Promised Land, the actual name of the community of his grandfather's youth. He almost seems to be avoiding direct conversation; the reader is surprised to learn that "I'd never spent this much time alone with my father. Seven hours and counting" (34). Guzzio has written of "some pathology, some inability for these men to break down the walls that separate them. Conversation of any kind can barely get into those silent spaces."[9] Wideman rattles off a list of facts about his father's life, then ends the first essay with the feeling that there is much work to do before that list can yield a portrait adequate to display his father accurately, just as there had been work to do with Robby in *Brothers and Keepers* to get beyond their initial awkward silences.

The journey continues in the next essay, "Fatheralong," which is largely about time and which plays with the connection between memoir and memory. John's earliest memory of his father recalls a parade in the snow. The details are fuzzy, but he definitely remembers riding home on the trolley with only his mother and concludes that his father must have gone to work at one of his jobs, which leads him to another memory of meeting his father at the restaurant where he worked in a department store. That meeting stands out because it was one of the few times John spent alone with Edgar. His general recollections reveal a father who was working too hard at eccentric hours to allow for much meaningful contact between them. He privately tries to figure out his own masculine identity by exploring territory beyond the domestic space defined by the maternal figures in his life. He sees this behavior as "flight" and interprets it as a search for his father rather than rebellion against his mother and other female elders: "Not so much deserting or shaming the women, as it was seeking [Edgar]. Loyalty the flip side of betrayal" (49). The gulf between men and women is like other binary definitions of difference he identifies throughout his writings, and he feels his role is to bridge this gulf: "Maybe I could come and go between my mother's world and my father's world, close the gap separating them" (50). But he is clearly somewhat guilty and anxious about this possibility, especially since the world where he seeks his father is a tawdry one of women in seedy bars.

His parents' separate worlds also account for a persistent tension in his writings between individualism and connection; he writes, "The first rule of my father's world is that you stand alone. Alone, alone, alone" (50), and "My mother's first rule was love. She refused to believe she was alone" (51). His father's tough pragmatism leads him to believe in and rely on nothing; his mother is motivated by her faith in God and family. Both of these convictions have their appeal, but John is unable to find common ground between them, and he views his inability to "maintain a foot in both worlds" as a letdown: "Neither Father's son nor Mother's son, betraying them both as I became myself. My mother's open arms. My father's arms crossed on his chest" (52). The process of becoming is painful here, and though it allows John the distance to be able to analyze his loved ones in depth, it also serves to alienate him. He becomes comfortable with allowing his father (like God the Father) to remain in some vague, absent space. When they do interact, in one particular scene that sticks in John's memory, it is not pleasant. When John calls his father a "spoor," a word he gleans from reading Tarzan books without fully understanding its meaning, Edgar hits him hard enough for John to remember the sensation years later. He is justifiably angry at his father's unmeasured response but also at how his father had manipulated language: "The trickiness of words, the ownership of words was tied up with this confusion and menace" (61). What for many children would have been a simple rite of passage—the sense of injustice that one's father has the power to discipline one brutally and unfairly and to call it a "love tap" (59)—is for John a complex inquiry into the nature of storytelling, interpretation, and rhetorical (as well as physical) control.

In fact, he goes so far as to connect his own story to patterns in mythology: "Father stories are about establishing origins and through them legitimizing claims of ownership, of occupancy and identity" (63). It is the act of storytelling that prevents death by preserving and revitalizing the lives of one's predecessors, whether or not they are heroic in the traditional sense. He turns from mythology to contemporary culture, one in which "black men, deprived of the voices of their fathers, are for all intents and purposes born semi-orphans" (65). He speaks even more specifically of prison as the compromised site where black fathers and sons meet in contemporary America and admits that his father does not visit Robby in prison because it is safer emotionally to preserve a kind of wall around the self. He reads outward from this situation to formulate a cultural critique of the "corrupted versions of [America's] institutions and values produced by the paradigm of race" (66), connecting back to his discussion in the introductory essay. Because of the unprecedented power of the mass media, the ancient practice of fearing the "other" has reached epidemic proportions: "Difference becomes deviance becomes division becomes demonization" (67). This simplistic thinking is destructive to a pluralistic society, and for Wideman it lies at the heart of the personal trials he and his loved ones endure. "The cloud of *race*" (69) affects parent-child relationship from the moment of birth. The father of a black child experiences a myriad of conflicting sensations when he realizes his child will have to face the same social battles he faced: "You are your son's biological link to past and future. Are you also his burden" (70). He claims this entire meditation is like a story—invented rather than drawn from actual experience, possible but not representative. Bringing in Richard Wright's autobiography as a point of comparison, he contemplates the real and present danger of racial self-loathing when one confronts the inadequacies of one's father. Wright (like Wideman) went into exile and into art as a way of becoming one's own father, "[creating] a world and its inhabitants" (74). The danger of racial self-loathing is a cancerous byproduct of any way of thinking that is based on race.

But black "orphans" or semi-orphans have other choices: to try to please their white fathers (Clarence Thomas) or to figuratively murder their white fathers (Malcolm X). Other possibilities include complete withdrawal and self-birth (Ellison's Invisible Man) or forming familial bonds with one's peers (street gangs). Wideman builds on this analysis to include history and culture back to the Renaissance, which coincided with the Western "discovery" of the African other. The logic of the Enlightenment was based on binary thinking, including the paradigm of race: "If Africa had not existed, Europe would have invented her. And did" (80). Miraculously, he manages to bring the essay back to his relationship to his parents in the its final pages, but the expansiveness of his thinking is impressive and sets the precedent for his future nonfiction in his ability to play with language, to allude to literature, to trace broad historical patterns, and finally to illustrate general truths through particular experiences.

Having built a vast intellectual framework for thinking through his trip with his father to South Carolina, Wideman is able to record details from that trip in the next essay, "Littleman." The title refers to his father's first cousin, who is a living link to their ancestral past since he remembers the death of Wideman's great-great-grandfather. Their excursion to the South to locate their family origins is a series of unofficial folkways to a place (Promised Land, a black community absent from most maps, referred to as "Promiseland" in Wideman's later book *Writing to Save a Life*) that exists apart from, even despite, official stories and documents. John, reminiscent of Milkman Dead in Toni Morrison's *Song of Solomon,* initially has trouble reading or appreciating the speech of southern people, and he becomes impatient with his father's way of connecting with a certain elderly man, a connection that produces Littleman, who is himself a direct connection to the past. Wideman is clearly setting himself up as someone who needs to learn a lesson during this journey. As he had needed to develop his "Homewood ear" in *Brothers and Keepers,* here he needs to develop a new ear to listen to his father and to his southern relatives and quasi relatives.

He comes to regard the South as one version of his home and history as a force "driven by mind" (102) more than anything fixed or stable. He learns to listen to the South itself in the same way he cultivates a new way of listening to southern people, and his imagination opens up to allow deep empathy, even identification, with the ghosts of those who have passed before him. This identification creates space for another meditation on the paradigm of race: the idea that history repeats itself is yet more proof of how deeply entrenched the paradigm is. He begins to distrust his own skeptical readings of southern hospitality: his deep belief is that the paradigm did not go away when slavery was abolished. He experiences a violent wave of anger when a cheerful, helpful white history professor aids him in his search for his ancestors by helping him navigate archives. The official documents the professor produces enrage Wideman because they are evidence of "the solid, banal, everyday business-as-usual role slavery played in America's past" (116). He moves past this anger so as to appreciate his father: to listen to stories of his past and to imagine that the two of them still have a story together as they drink beer with Littleman, eating fish and contemplating a bar fight that never happens. He sees this macho fantasy as "silliness" but acknowledges "something rich and good about being with men of my family" (126).

The penultimate essay, "Picking Up My Father at the Springfield Station," continues the story of the South Carolina journey while combining it with the journey described in the title. Edgar is presented as a deposed king, overlooked (or deliberately left behind) by John's extended family when they sojourned from Pittsburgh to Amherst for John's son's wedding. As John drives to meet him at the train station, he is certain of one thing: that Edgar will not let on that his family's neglect hurts him. John is aware that he has inherited his father's taciturn indifference: "Wasn't I his son in all this, his twin mirrored on the glass wall separating us when we spoke?" (134). This question echoes the similarities as well as the barriers between himself and Robby in *Brothers and Keepers*. Despite his efforts to open up, the task remains difficult as masculine toughness is part of his genetic makeup. He admits how close to his father he is in terms of sensibility despite the fact that his mother was present throughout his upbringing while his father was absent. The freedom his father sought when he ultimately left his family is something John desires, and he concludes this of his father and of all fathers: "He can't always take you with him, but you will follow in his footsteps" (141). Throughout the book Wideman has addressed the African concept of "Great Time" in which past, present, and future merge. In this essay he effectively collapses time and space in mental journeys that unite him and his father, and that bridge the gap between various visits, from the origin quest in South Carolina to a prison visit to Arizona. Indirectly, for the first time, he acknowledges the incarceration of his son Jacob, imprisoned since 1986 for murder.

Just as quickly, he changes the subject, again mirroring his father's unwillingness to visit his son Robby in prison. The trip to South Carolina and to the bus station late at night become connected in his mind, the dingy station emblematic of the place where black fathers and sons are destined to meet in America. These seedy streets peopled with prostitutes, cops, and criminals are the streets where John had sought out his father as a youth. Now he exercises his freedom by entering a tawdry strip club, which he acknowledges is one of his secret pleasures, though he often loathes the experience and leaves in shame and embarrassment. The level of confession is high here as Wideman confronts his motivations for participating in this exploitative business and admits that race is a factor, as he has only ever encountered one black dancer in the club and his response to her was to avert his eyes in shame. When his father arrives, there is no tension between them: John has apparently confronted his demons privately. Upon closer examination, though, he has barely encountered them at all: the brief mention of Jacob's incarceration is buried under the tale of this much less traumatic secret.

The wedding involves a repetition as Edgar is left behind once again at his hotel and misses the ceremony, though he makes it to the reception afterward. But John, waiting for his father to arrive, experiences extreme consternation because his absence from this ceremony is the culmination of a lifetime of absences: "My father stuck somewhere losing this moment was lost to me. I mourned him" (174). In the next breath, however, he draws on his ability to avoid sentimentality in order to move on—a trait he learned or inherited from his father.

The final essay, "Father Stories," is addressed to Jacob, Wideman's incarcerated son, but the reader must work hard to figure out the identity of the "you" in the essay because the author remains reluctant to discuss his son and never names him in this work. The vignettes within the essay are sometimes inventive and deliberately unorganized: "I'm remembering things in no order, with no plan. These father stories. Because that's all they are" (184). This final sentence sounds dismissive, but father stories, as the entire book has proven, are crucial to self-discovery, to familial and racial continuity, and to any examined life, even when they do not seem particularly profound or conclusive. Time has been the subject of many of the essays in this memoir, and memory plays an important role: "Memory then isn't so much archival as it is a seeking of vitality/harmony, an evocation of a truer, more complete, saturated present tense. All this of course relates to personality—the construction of a continuous narrative of self. Our stories. Father stories" (187). Many of these stories are simply memories of what might be said to constitute some bedrock of Jacob's personality: the way he would clutch his mother's hair, his fear of leaves, an anecdote about him stealing the keys to a truck when he was four or five. The essay approaches Jacob's incarceration obliquely: twice Wideman refers to his life sentence as "that summer you never came back" (191), and his crime is described as "hearing you were missing and a boy found dead in the room the two of you had been sharing" (192). Wideman acknowledges his pain virtually at the end of the book, but the reader becomes aware that it had been there all along, informing all the essays with a weight and urgency that had been palpable, if not explained: "I felt myself coming apart, the mask I'd been wearing, as much for myself as for the benefit of other people, was beginning to splinter" (192). In a moment of intense grief, he falls to the ground, alone, and rubs his face with dirt. This is one of many moments that have defined the seven years his son has been in prison. The essay ends with a brief reflection on what he knows of his ancestry, what has been limited by American history and culture (produced by the race paradigm), and the crucial value of stories to foster the difficulty of survival.

In a 1995 interview essay, Patricia Smith wrote, "Wideman refuses to speak of Jacob directly, although the memory of his youngest is evident and pervasive. In his hands. The gently cracking voice. The slamming of his eyes." In the same essay the author described the way "Wideman abruptly detaches himself, turns a personal hurt into a world lesson."[10] This pattern can be seen in his nonfiction about his family and himself: the principle of illustrating the general through the particular informs all his prose, but moreover, there is a delicate dance between the emotional and visceral on one side and the intellectual and analytical on the other. We might regard him as a physician who cuts into himself for the benefit of those in the operating theater but who is conscious of his need to survive the scalpel. His wounds are evident, but we are not invited to regard them too closely.

Taken together, these two family memoirs mark an important crossroads in Wideman's work. As much as the Homewood novels, these works blend confession and invention, and the memoir form enables him to showcase his unique brand of layered analysis while developing his concerns with memory, family, storytelling, and survival.

CHAPTER 5

Enter Philadelphia

Although Pittsburgh is the primary location of Wideman's work, during his middle years he put that city into conversation with Philadelphia, the city where he attended college. Two historical events—the yellow fever epidemic of 1792 and the police bombing of the MOVE compound in 1985—provided Wideman with much raw material for his fiction during the late 1980s and 1990s. Professionally, this was a tremendously successful period in Wideman's career, including his receiving a PEN/Faulkner Award in 1990 and a MacArthur Grant in 1993. Personally, it was an especially tragic one, bracketed by the arrest of his son Jacob in 1986 and the end of his marriage in 2000.

A 1991 interviewer identified a "new experimentalism" in Wideman's work, and he responded, "writing's always been a matter of taking chances and pushing a form, as well as pushing my own development within the form."[1] During this period he was pushing particularly hard, especially in his willingness to obliterate the boundaries between genres. In a 1993 interview, responding to a question about the difference between nonfiction, reportage, and fiction, he said, "I don't think there is much difference. I think, for instance, historians are probably novelists who haven't come out of the closet."[2] This position has given him considerable flexibility and range. Through his prominence, he had arrived at a podium that he sometimes chose to use to make pronouncements about his culture (as in a 1992 *Esquire* article that developed out of the Rodney King riots in Los Angeles or in his 1996 foreword to *Live from Death Row,* a memoir by Mumia Abu-Jamal, the prominent imprisoned journalist) and just as often chose not to use, pointing to the differences between fiction and sociology.[3]

Wideman's middle novels demonstrate his maturing aesthetic and a philosophical toughness and complexity he had developed in his nonfiction. In fact, there are strong nonfictional elements in these works—not just the autobiography that underpins them but actual passages where the author's personae dissolve and we see Wideman himself in the same light in which he revealed (and occasionally concealed) himself in *Brothers and Keepers* and *Fatheralong.* Readers might be tempted to call these works postmodern in contrast with his first three novels, which borrowed heavily from high modernism, but these works share only some of postmodernism's characteristics (such as self-reflexiveness and clever wordplay) while eschewing others (such as a reaction to technological terror and absurdist humor). If there is a consistent subject in these four novels, it is the writer's struggle to understand, to write into (if not through) despair, and to invent new ways to describe his world. These works are opportunities for Wideman to ruminate on broad subjects by concentrating on specific characters and events, not unlike his third novel *The Lynchers.* In *Reuben* (1987) the reader pays special attention to the title character, but Reuben is really the conduit to a place (Homewood, again) and to the way generations in that place are in a constant state of negotiation and disagreement, an enduring theme in Wideman's work. Reuben is only one principal character, but he unites the tale as he is both a mythmaker and the subject of others' mythology. The effect of this focus is to decenter the work, making it one of Wideman's most challenging.

Reuben is a street lawyer who defends the poor. He is connected to his community but slightly apart from it like Cecil in *Hurry Home* ("another of Wideman's alienated intellectuals,"[4] in Guzzio's words). His education makes him a respected figure, but it also opens him up for ridicule, and many of the Homewood residents make fun of his foreshortened physique and quirky facial hair. In the first chapter Kwansa Parker approaches him to help recover her lost son Cudjoe, who had been taken away from her because she is deemed an unfit mother. She tells her story: how her lover Waddell impregnated her, left her, and became involved with dope. He has now cleaned up and married a woman who encourages him to take Cudjoe back. Reuben claims that they have no case since Kwansa has raised the boy. She feels that her body and mind are separating, and it is a familiar sensation because she also experiences it when she trades sexual favors for money. This dissociation of an individual self—the schism between internal and external lives—is a recurrent motif in *Reuben.* It allows the book to diverge from the main line of its narrative into flights of the imagination that seem like distractions but are actually the substance of the tale. While listening to Reuben, Kwansa skates off into her memory, recalling youths in the public library reciting Robert Hayden's poem "Middle Passage," or watching women consulting a Ouija board, or judging her own unfeeling reaction to a local homeless woman succumbing to despair on a cold winter's day. Cudjoe is the reason she herself doesn't succumb to despair: "Her son had saved her. . . . Touching him, touch lived again" (13). Her quest to recover Cudjoe, then, is a quest for salvation.

Reuben is fascinated by Eadweard Muybridge, the pioneering nineteenth-century photographer who was obsessed with capturing motion on film. Muybridge provides a metaphor for Reuben's tendency toward paralysis in old age: he concentrates on individual pieces of evidence, such as Muybridge's individual frames, but has a more difficult time translating them into the pattern of motion they constitute. As the narrator describes it more deeply, though, Muybridge's art begins to resemble Wideman's developing aesthetic: "Freezing things into unnatural frames. Forestalling an inevitable conclusion by the logic of another conclusion, just as inevitable if the dice are given a slightly different spin" (17). Wideman's tendency is to ask "what if?" and work through a number of possibilities for a given set of circumstances or trains of thought that an individual character might pursue. Reuben is drawn to coincidence and connections. He tries to make sense of his two obsessions—with Muybridge and with the ancient Egyptians—as they both comment on the nature of time. Mummification and photography are not only ways to preserve the past but to reanimate it in the future. The bodies of Muybridge's subjects are alive for Reuben in the same way the Egyptians sought to preserve the bodies of the living for eternity. It is unclear whether such philosophical wanderings will help Kwansa get her son back, but it is clear that Reuben is invested in their story because it represents to him a renewal of his own waning life forces.

The topic of aging comes up explicitly in the next section in a conversation between Reuben and the chapter title character, Wally, a basketball recruiter with fantasies that tend to racial violence and rough misogyny. Wally seeks Reuben not for legal counsel but for wisdom. He contemplates identity deeply, regarding the clothes he packs to travel as potential disguises and meditating on his feelings of alienation. Reality is a problem for Wally: his fantasies of smashing white heads on a plane with a baseball bat yields to a story he tells of the first time he murdered a white man, without provocation, in a public restroom somewhere on his travels. Reuben questions whether the story is true, and Wally realizes that the details of it are imprecise in his memory. Reuben encourages him to fill in some details, "For the sake of the story. For your sake. For fun" (45). Wally takes this advice as an insult, but it is another commentary on Wideman's developing aesthetic, one in which the writer's imagination and impulse to create take precedence over verifiable facts.

Yet the imagination is not always beneficial. Kwansa spends an afternoon drinking gin with a woman named Toodles, who becomes her lover. When she goes to pick up Cudjoe, she learns that his father, Waddell, has arrived first, and

Cudjoe's absence causes Kwansa to overindulge in her fears of the boy's death. Perhaps this response is what Reuben is trying to avoid. In the next chapter he engages in a dialogue with Muybridge's ghost on the subject of time and immortality. Again, commenting on Wideman's aesthetic, Muybridge tells Reuben that the two of them could "let go of our stony notions of starts, stops, beginnings, middles, ends" (63), indicating the African principle of "Great Time" that Wideman repeatedly references in his nonfiction. Complicating the notion of time, Reuben carries a gold watch with a small figure attached to it that represents his twin brother, taken from him at birth. He calls this brother "Reuben" and invents or dreams scenarios about his life, reinforcing the theme of multiple identities that permeates the novel. Pointedly, in one of these stories, his brother is in jail, and "Reuben would need all the days of his life to examine the black cell, become acquainted with the brother sealed there" (66). The totem of his brother is related to a totem he manufactures out of some junk he has gathered, and he imagines it to control the fate of Kwansa and Cudjoe. He suffers a crisis of confidence, calling himself "Mountebank. Charlatan. Fool. Witch doctor" (71). He recalls how he had once been an object of ridicule in Philadelphia, and the novel changes gears again.

In Philadelphia, Reuben had been the porter, or "mascot" (73), for a group of white fraternity brothers who would occasionally sojourn to a black brothel run by a tough prostitute named Flora. One day the boys "purchase" Flora for Reuben, but instead of having sex, the two of them have a long conversation about what they really think of the boys. Reuben has been using his position at the fraternity to study law. Flora is contemptuous of the fraternity boys. The scene turns grisly: the fraternity boys, hooded and drunk as at a lynching, burst in on the scene and physically torment both Flora and Reuben, repeating their conversation and reminding them of the hierarchy in which they are at the bottom. They whip Reuben and are about to assault Flora when they realize that the piano player downstairs has lit the place on fire. Flora and the piano player are killed in the inferno, and Reuben is tossed to the pavement, rendering him unconscious for a week. This horrific episode silently defines his life thereafter. Reuben temporarily represses the memory, but it has become "entirely, eternally" his again (89). He tells the story to Wally, who is as skeptical of it as Reuben had been of Wally's tale of wanton murder. Even though Wally had come to Reuben on business, he finds himself transfixed by the tale of Flora, whether it is technically "true" or not: "The old dude was loony but he told good lies. . . . Just enough fact and detail to trick you into almost believing them" (90). But Wally misinterprets the story, according to Reuben: it is supposed to be about loss, not about the anger that should engender revenge. Philadelphia becomes a metaphor for Reuben: "All black men have a Philadelphia. Part of you. A brother trapped there forever" (93). In other words, all black men have a site or incident of trauma. The "trapped brother" evokes not only Reuben's totem, which he carries on his watch, but also Wideman's brother Robby. Revenge is too simple an emotion to describe Reuben's or Wideman's reaction to an unfair world.

Although Wally expresses the need for revenge when Reuben tells the story of Flora, Wally's actual response to the unfairness of the world is detachment. Like the other characters, he has a tendency to separate his mind and his body, especially as he goes about his business of recruiting young black basketball players for his university. The practice reminds him of slavery, and the only way he can overcome his moral repugnance is to "treat what he was doing as if it was happening to someone else" (102). This strategy may preserve him, but it also results in an identity crisis that alienates him, revealing a misogynistic streak that prevents emotional closeness with women. We learn that Wally's personal Philadelphia is in fact Philadelphia, when he was at the University of Pennsylvania on a basketball scholarship, just like his creator. Wally shared the same feelings of isolation that Wideman expresses in *Brothers and Keepers*. He became despondent at his realization that he would never fit in with the wealthy white students around him: "If the game was set up so you could never win . . . if you'd never be one of them, why play?" (111). His experience has led to self-loathing: "I learned to hate the face in the mirror. My own face. Hate it for giving in, hate it for not being the right one, hate it for hating itself" (112). This schism within him further destabilizes the story he told Reuben about murdering a white man. In a new iteration of the story, the crime was committed not by him but by another black recruiter who had developed a philosophy of "abstract hate" of white people to justify homicide of a random white individual. By the end of "The Recruiter" chapter, the line between reality and fantasy is completely blurred. The act of telling stories is the key to navigating these worlds. Wally is trying to make his story believable to his auditor, Reuben, as when one recounts a dream: "Whether his story makes sense or not to you, he believes it. So a door's open. And once he steps through and takes you by the hand with him, you can't argue about what's on the other side. Cause there you are. Through the door. It's real" (122). The recruiter in the airplane seat next to Wally is a shape shifter, a projection of his imagination that shares some of his features, not unlike Wideman's fictional creations. His aesthetic involves altering the details of his experience to allow his imagination, sometimes grotesquely, to produce a new reality. Reuben similarly meditates on the nature of his own divided self, trying to use Muybridge to make sense of it. He wonders if his memory is reliable, if his progress through the world as he perceives it constitutes identity, or even consciousness.

It should be clear that the plot of the book—Reuben's attempts to help Wally and Kwansa with their legal woes—is not its most compelling feature. (Reviewer Noel Perrin claimed that "*Reuben* has no real plot—just events, told discontinuously," and argued that these features are less important than Wideman's mesmerizing voice, "building sound, not story.")[5] Wideman's emphasis is on the way individual minds react to experience. The tendency to divide oneself, to separate mind from body, and to question reality all create opportunities for complex storytelling, which is Wideman's stock-in-trade. Kwansa, for her part, wants to believe that there's a better self within her. Her personal "Philadelphia"—the incident that deeply affected her and caused her self-loathing—is the death of her grandmother, Big Mama, whose Christian faith caused her to beat Kwansa as a means of discipline, including when she became pregnant with Cudjoe. She feels guilt for resenting her grandmother and her faith, and as a result Cudjoe represents her good side. Her loss of him is akin to Reuben's loss of Flora, and both respond with a desperate attempt at love—but the kind that does not benefit the self.

Wally's tendency to divide himself is not always a way to displace his violent, murderous rage. He meditates on the other Wally he has created as he runs, and running is in fact a substitute for interactions with other humans as he consciously competes with himself. He recognizes the potency of the doubles he and Reuben have created: "If you killed your own sure enough double you'd be alone" (170). This anxiety betrays Wally's underlying problem: that he *is* alone, that he has isolated himself from all the women in his life, that he is orphaned, and that his best friend, who has been paralyzed in an accident, has asked for his help in committing suicide. Reuben is his only friend, and Wally immediately recognizes the irony when the odd little lawyer calls him to bail him out of jail when Wally is the one who has committed a crime (which may only be a fantasy). Reuben's "crime" is that he has been operating as a lawyer without the proper credentials: he is called an "impostor" in a newspaper report, heightening the novel's concerns with reality and identity. Both Reuben and the reader have a difficult time sorting out dream from reality, or imagination from actual circumstances, as the novel concludes, but its final dramatic scene—of Kwansa and her lover, Toodles, killing Waddell in a bar fight—seems to have actually happened because it is narrated in the voice of an eyewitness. The lost boy, Cudjoe, is located at last and Reuben arrives to take him home. Still, much of the novel's conflicts are unresolved because they are deeply embedded within the consciousness of each of the three main characters.

The name Cudjoe figures prominently in Wideman's next novel, *Philadelphia Fire* (1990), but there's no indication that the missing boy from *Reuben* is the same character. Historically, Cudjoe was a Jamaican leader of a group of runaway slaves known as the Maroons. He was famous for leading attacks on sugar plantations. Stories of Cudjoe smack of legend: he was a Robin Hood–like figure who managed to outwit the technologically superior British colonial forces to liberate the oppressed. In *Philadelphia Fire* the figure of Cudjoe is the alter-ego of the author: a sometime reporter covering the aftermath of the Philadelphia police attack on the MOVE organization in 1985. MOVE was a localized black liberation movement founded in 1972 by a man named John Africa (born Vincent Leapheart), who had a series of run-ins with the police. Like the characters in *Reuben,* Wideman feels a split within himself between the emotionally distant writer and the social activist who would respond publicly to the injustice he witnesses. In a startling move Wideman's nonfiction voice arrives in the pages of this novel, temporarily replacing the fictional persona Cudjoe and further blurring the line between real life and stories.

Philadelphia Fire begins with a meditation on names and the divided worlds that individual characters can inhabit. Cudjoe is on a boat in the Greek Isles with Zivanias, a man whose name alludes to native moonshine whiskey. Ruminating on their names, Cudjoe is able to traverse space mentally, from the distant Greek site of his vacation to Philadelphia, where he has returned in the aftermath of the police attack on the MOVE compound. As in *Reuben,* there is a lost child in this novel, one who is unaccounted for after the police bombing. Cudjoe is unsure why he is so desperate to find the child; it is as though the boy completes him. Like Wideman and various personae he has created, Cudjoe is anxious about his credibility within the black community; when he meets the survivors of the attack on MOVE, he thinks, "how, after the briefest of conversations, did they know his history, that he married a white woman and fathered half-white kids? How did they know he'd failed his wife and failed those kids, that his betrayal was double, about blackness and about being a man?" (9–10). Based on an interview with one of the women from MOVE, Margaret Jones, it is clear that the organization may be misguided and cult-like, but it definitely interrogates the meaning of "blackness." Margaret refers to herself and others as "slaves" to their leader but claims that he tells a certain kind of uncomfortable truth that is related to their race. She wonders why there hasn't been any real progress for generations and questions whether the Christian church truly has the salvation of black people in mind. She also wonders why Cudjoe is so obsessed with young Simba, "Simmie," the boy who disappeared. "The truth is, I'm not really sure," he answers (19). Cudjoe is Wideman's alter-ego, so it is fair to extrapolate that the unspoken answer has to do with Wideman's brother Robby and son Jacob, both lost in their own way into the prison system.

The bombing of the MOVE compound is really more of a catalyst for the novel than its true subject. The subject is the struggle of the writer to produce writing that is honest and original. Cudjoe continues to move back and forth over space and time, and in a passage that reveals much about Wideman's aesthetic, he says, "he must always write about many places at once. No choice. The splitting apart is inevitable. First step is always out of time, away from responsibility, toward the word or sound or image that is everywhere at once, that connects and destroys" (23). In the case of *Philadelphia Fire,* the place indicated in the title is important, but it does not confine the novel. "Fire" is more important as the image that draws the author, sends him running in pursuit of the missing child who has escaped the fire. There is a palpable sense of urban decay that applies not only to Philadelphia and Pittsburgh but that follows Cudjoe/Wideman on his travels around the world. When Cudjoe travels to Clark Park for a second interview with Margaret Jones, he spends as much time reminiscing about his earlier experiences there—including plenty of basketball and some journaling in front of a statue of Dickens—as he does talking with Margaret. He decides to join a basketball game, and it highlights the theme of his conversation with Margaret: that things have gotten worse in the neighborhood. The basketball is not as good as it once was, Cudjoe learns about old friends who are in prison or otherwise diminished, and dope dealers are more prominent than dedicated hoop players. Still, in the quiet following an evening of hard ball playing, he bonds with the other men and learns their perspective on both the MOVE bombing and the missing boy. As in *Brothers and Keepers* he has to train himself to listen and allow stories to get told in their own way.

Detachment is what makes Cudjoe's job possible. He connects to the residents of Philadelphia but just as quickly removes himself from them to allow his imagination and observations to shape his world. He thinks of himself as a journalist with no connection to Philadelphia, then wonders if what he is writing is a detective story as opposed to some other kind of fictional nonfiction. In his detached state he is able both to recall his own past and to project himself into the MOVE compound on the night of the bombing. He lingers on one particular episode from his past: a trip with his family to an island, where he gives a manuscript to his editor, Sam. The trip is fraught with significance as Cudjoe recalls his sexual frustration since he and his wife are denied privacy while dealing with their kids. He spies Sam's daughter Cassandra cavorting naked in the moonlight and indulges in a sexual fantasy about her even though Sam is his friend and Cassandra is only eighteen. The fantasy is severely compromised in Cudjoe's memory because he now knows that Cassandra died nine months later in a car crash, and Sam is dead as well. He credits Sam with one of the aphorisms that, again, serves as a fair assessment of Wideman's aesthetic: "technique . . . is truth" (64). The truth of Wideman's stories is in the way they examine possibilities rather than accepting the way things appear to be on the surface.

The deaths of Cassandra and Sam intensify the novel's theme of loss, and Cudjoe attempts to overcome his detachment by describing how he has lost his wife and children: "He'd removed himself absolutely from their lives" (69). His detachment explains how he can move on beyond this separation, and it also explains his tendency to go into exile: "That's what he couldn't face. The mirror in her eyes. The hurt. The truth. Run. Run" (70). It may seem that we are a long way from the fire of the title, but Wideman's readers must learn to be patient and flexible as they are seeking connections. It is important to recall that Cudjoe was in exile in Greece at the beginning of the novel and that he is drawn back to Philadelphia through the vehicle of memory to the conflagration in his personal life. The subject of the novel turns back to the fire as Cudjoe interviews Timbo, an old friend from his days at the university, who is now an assistant to the black mayor who authorized the attack on the MOVE compound. Timbo is an apologist for the mayor and tries to emphasize how much better the city has become, but as their conversation continues, he gradually acknowledges that its prosperity only applies to some and that the MOVE residents had to be eradicated because they were politically embarrassing. Cudjoe is depressed listening to Timbo, who has become cynical, believing that everyone is motivated by nothing more than greed, but in speaking to him Cudjoe confesses something about his own story, how he spent a decade in exile on Mykonos and failed to write the novel about the 1960s (featuring Timbo and others) that he had always meant to write. The ending of this section blurs the line between reality and dream. After Timbo and Cudjoe discuss the rise of a gang of kids who call themselves MPT ("Money Power Things"), Cudjoe reveals a nightmare he has had in which he hears kids singing, then discovers a lynched child hanging from a basketball hoop. This grotesque imagery brings together many of the troubles on Cudjoe's mind, all involving loss. He is left paralyzed, unable to invent the connections that will make sense of the dream. Cudjoe's condition is the artist's dilemma, the paralysis he feels when he experiences a changing world and does not know what to do with it.

Part 2 of the novel does not seem like a novel at all but rather a trademark Wideman miscellany of quotations and observations endemic to his nonfiction works. Cudjoe even disappears and is replaced by Wideman himself, describing the moment when he and his wife watched the news story of the Philadelphia fire on television. He also reveals the incarceration of his son Jacob, with which he dealt so tentatively in *Fatheralong*. When John learns about the fire, he is channel surfing with his wife, Judy, as they lie on their bed in Wyoming. Stylistically, this section resembles that channel surfing as the author moves rapidly across time and space, revealing his own wounds and fleeing from them instantly, including snippets from a journal as well as an analysis of Shakespeare's final play, *The Tempest* (which becomes a recurrent touchstone in Wideman's oeuvre, even, as Ulrich Eschborn put it, "the most important intertextual reference in [his] work"[6]). The subject of multiple selves is revealed explicitly as Wideman meditates on his son's circumstances in prison: "he must live many lives at once, yet have no life except the chaos produced by divided, warring selves. The utter frustration, loneliness and fear accompanying such an awareness are incomprehensible" (110). He has internalized his son's condition and feels himself both divided and perpetually sad. The invention of fictional personae and the stories that accompany them are clearly ways to avoid being mired in this sadness. And yet he wonders whether he can ever write his son's story, and the result of this wondering is more paralysis. The very fact of Jacob's incarceration is a trap for his identity as a writer. He wonders not only whether he can write about it but also whether he should. The repercussions of Jacob's imprisonment are profound: "A child lost cancels the natural order, the circle is broken" (119). It is about more than ancestry: the psychological wholeness of individuals and groups depends upon the natural order.

The Tempest functions as a prism through which to bend his life. He renders Caliban as a Jamaican with dreadlocks, and the reader might conclude that Caliban must be Cudjoe, but this Caliban indicates that Wideman is Prospero: "Take ebryting. . . . Go off teach at University. Write book. . . . Steal from breddar. Steal from son" (121). Their stories of incarceration become the subjects of Wideman's books just as Prospero (whose magic was also books) stole the island from Caliban and attempted to rename everything on it. The author's guilt is palpable. He breaks the fourth wall: "Why this Cudjoe, then? This airy other floating into the shape of my story. Why am I him when I tell certain parts? Why am I hiding from myself? Is he mirror or black hole?" (122). There are no explicit answers to these questions, but the implication is that Wideman can only write, indeed can only survive, if he creates such personae. When writing about MOVE he expresses the same anxieties revealed in his attempts to write about his brother and son, and he again becomes Prospero rather than Cudjoe but pivots again to become a fast-talking interpreter of Shakespeare, who not only translates the bard but explains his "con." Wideman imagines this scene as the introduction to what he calls "the central event" in the book, a "production of *The Tempest* staged by Cudjoe in the late late 1960s" (132). It is an event that was planned but did not actually come about, and it is the key to understanding all the book's many concerns, from the urban fire, to the incarcerated son, to the despairing, laboring writer. The play, though it never happened, gave urban schoolchildren a chance to rethink their own lives, and this section ends with the author speaking directly to his son with advice that stems from this same lesson: "We don't know what the future will bring.

We do have a chance to unfold our days one by one and piece together a story that shapes us" (151).

Part 3 of the novel switches gears again, focusing on one James Brown (J.B. for short) whose story is interspersed with that of a rapper named Rapcity. Both are focused on the burning city of Philadelphia. J.B. is a protean figure, an educated man who lives on the streets and does not know where he fits in. He is isolated and more than once alludes to Ellison's *Invisible Man*. There is a war raging between young and old, and J.B. does not know whose side he is on. There are two main plot points in this section: his girlfriend, Cynthia, is attacked by a gang of youths as they exit a cinema (causing J.B. to feel shame rather than empathy), and a white businessman jumps to his death from a skyscraper. The suicidal man had been holding a briefcase containing a pistol, which J.B. picks up when no one is looking. While J.B. is sleeping on the streets, some youths drench him in kerosene and light him on fire. This senseless conflagration sets up the final scene in which Cudjoe attends a public memorial service for the victims of the MOVE bombing. Cudjoe is at first paralyzed by the ceremony, not understanding how to feel as mourners release balloons and hold candles. In the end he senses a howling mob comprising figures from throughout history calling his name as he silently intones the words "*Never again*" (199). He turns to face this mob, and although it is unclear what will happen next, it is clear that Cudjoe sees the necessity of confronting difficult truths. The speakers at the service have responded across the spectrum from forgiveness to revenge, but what comes through in Cudjoe's final epiphany is a recognition of the inevitability of pain.

Philadelphia Fire is considered one of Wideman's more off-putting works despite its winning the PEN/Faulkner award. Discussing the way "breaks, fissures, and gaps" function in Wideman's work, Guzzio wrote, "*Philadelphia Fire*'s narrative structure ultimately fractures from the gaps, to the extent that it seems to have alienated many critics as well as readers,"[7] alluding to reviews by Ishmael Reed and Charles Johnson. (In a 1991 interview Wideman revealed his respect for these fellow novelists but claimed that they both "missed the point in the same way," as they seemed to want a book that was more of an indictment of the MOVE bombing. Interestingly, in a 1994 interview, Reed singled out *Philadelphia Fire* as "one of the most remarkable books.")[8] Dorothea Mbalia, in one of the first book-length studies of Wideman, praised the book as a turning point in which the author embraces a "newfound Africanness" that unlocked his imagination.[9] Susan Pearsall held up the novel as one that readers should take seriously even as she acknowledged Wideman's spotty reception: "Because of the relevance of its concerns, the urgency and distinctiveness of its voice, and its uniquely expressive narrative technique, *Philadelphia Fire* . . . deserves serious consideration."[10]

Reuben has had a similar fate, with reviews considering it inscrutable but academic critics giving it considerable attention. Upon its publication, Walter Kendrick criticized it while praising the Homewood Trilogy and *Brothers and Keepers.* The greatness of the earlier books lay in Wideman's gifts of observation rather than invention. He regarded *Reuben* as incoherent and tired, claiming that Homewood probably did not have any stories left that Wideman could use, and he hoped that *Reuben* "mark[ed] a pause for breath" rather than a downward trend in the author's career.[11] A quarter century after its publication, Byerman saw it as a continuation of the Homewood Trilogy, calling it "a novel about how the main characters struggle to do some good, while being aware of their imperfections. . . . they carry on the pattern of the Homewood trilogy in trying to find some reason to continue in a troubled world."[12]

Although *The Cattle Killing* (1996) connects to some of the developing themes and techniques in Wideman's career circa 1996, it marks a departure as well. Despite the postmodern framing at the beginning and end, it is largely a historical novel set in the eighteenth century. Although the setting is Philadelphia, the time period distinguishes it from other works such as *Philadelphia Fire,* and the cast of characters is larger than that of many of his works. Nonetheless, it is vintage Wideman in the way he trains his focus on a single event—the Xhosa's cattle killing as a way of avoiding European oppression—and reads outward from it so that the event is more an image than the book's true subject. Lisa Lynch acknowledged that this novel (and the related short story "Fever") are distinct from Wideman's other work, but also argued convincingly that "a concern with writing African Americans into history informs all of Wideman's writing."[13]

The novel begins with a lengthy italicized passage in which the author reflects on his youth while climbing the hill to visit his father, reminiscent of *Fatheralong,* with the decay of the modern city commenting on the image of the cattle killing: "*Black boys shoot each other. Murder themselves. . . .* The cattle are the people. The people are the cattle. . . . *The image haunts him. Xhosa killing their cattle, killing themselves, a world coming apart*" (7). This moment is the portal between the author's mind-set and the past: what felt like a self-protective action based on "an evil prophecy" (7) becomes self-destructive. He announces in no uncertain terms that he wants the image of the Xhosa killing their cattle—a reckless act based on a people following a false prophecy, ruining an ancient way of life—to resonate in the minds of his readers. He is conscious, as he was in *Philadelphia Fire,* that his work is "*True and not true (check out the facts, dates, murders). Not exactly a novel. Hybrid"* (8). Wideman's primary impulse is toward invention as a way of exposing a complex, difficult truth. He is also aware of the way he interacts with the various personae who people his books. To become their conduit, he fashions himself as an all-seeing character named "Eye," who can look at himself and his own father but also look back on history and outward from people relegated to that history.

As the novel proper begins, the reader senses that Wideman has time-traveled into his eighteenth-century subject's body. The initial passage is like awakening from a dream—by now a familiar motif in Wideman's storytelling—and the character is trying to discern the difference between reality and perception. He is a black preacher (unnamed,[14] referred to here as The Reverend) lost in the wilderness. He comes across a cabin in the woods and offers to work for food; the white inhabitant of the cabin accuses him of being the devil. He assures him he is not, proceeds to split wood, and suffers as a splinter enters his flesh. He then steals the ax, and his story becomes one he tells in the first person to an ailing woman before he retreats to the barn. The act of storytelling to a willing listener is ultimately more important than the factual truth of the tale, as had been the case in *Reuben*. Now in first-person narrative mode, he reveals that he had lived through a plague of fever destroying Philadelphia. He tells of how he had purchased freedom for himself, his mother, and his brother; but when they died, he turned to religion for comfort. When plague strikes, he and other black residents of Philadelphia are blamed for it even though they are as much its victims as whites are. He tells a woeful tale of a black mother carrying an infant who has died: he accompanies them to a lake, into which the mother carries the baby as a way of sending it on its journey to the afterlife, then drowns herself while The Reverend watches. The point of the story is the accumulation of images for the sake of the auditor, who is the ailing woman in the barn. She is eager to put together the story of the splintered wood and the drowning woman, and also anxious for the story to return to Philadelphia.

But the story, like many of Wideman's, is largely about the nature of storytelling itself, with a number of thematic elements to give it fuel: racial revenge, the death of innocents, and the role of destiny. The narrator has heard many versions of the story about the woman and infant he met along the road. Most of them involve a white landowner expelling the child in hopes of keeping the plague out of his house. Some of them include a dutiful black slave leaving with the child to protect it. In other versions the black woman is the child's mother. But the narrator chooses to believe the old African saying that Wideman appropriates so often: "all stories are true" (53). All are plausible and thus give rise to the imagination's capacity for invention. The circuitous path of stories is firmly established as part of his aesthetic by this point: "going backward in the story is more important than proceeding forward" (54). Moreover, all stories represent returns: "To memory, possibility, life" (55).

The Reverend occasionally has fits that could best be described as seizures, though he considers them opportunities for visions. There is a schism between the passionate, emotional celebrations he and others of African descent engage in to express their faith and the cool, disciplined style of European descendants. The racism implicit in this distinction forces The Reverend outdoors for his worship and onto the roads and byways, where he becomes an itinerant preacher. This experience opens his eyes to the nature of slavery, the wide variety of people considered both "white" and "black," and the way Christianity functions differently among different groups of people. Even though he is an ex-slave, he is keenly aware of the segregated nature of his world. When he is seized by the spirit (presumably one of his fits) in church, the white preacher drives him out as though he is a devil rather than the visionary prophet he claims to be. After he is banished, he nearly freezes to death in a snowstorm and is discovered by Liam Stubbs and his white wife, who take him into their bed to revive him. Mrs. Stubbs's method of reviving him is sexual, and she spends her next morning vaguely guilty and curious about her actions. When The Reverend awakens, however, she befriends him. Liam is also revived by The Reverend's presence. Liam had once been full of stories but had gradually gone silent. It is perhaps the presence of another man of African descent that has provided the key to his reanimation.

As Stubbs rediscovers his voice, the three are able to engage in deep storytelling and conversation. Mrs. Stubbs questions The Reverend's faith as she expresses her own skepticism about the benevolence of any god who would create such an unfair world. For his part, Stubbs tells of how he was forced to work in a tannery in England after being stolen from Africa. Recalling Wideman's early image of cattle killing, The Reverend tries to reconcile his faith in God with the brutality of men: "Beast blood, man blood, mingled on the knives, noises of men and beasts mixed indistinguishably" (111). Stubbs's goal is to educate The Reverend about his own condition. The truth is that he and Mrs. Stubbs pretend to be mistress and slave rather than husband and wife, and when Stubbs sells lumber, he pretends to do so at the behest of his supposed mistress.

Stubbs had distinguished himself in England by being smarter and harder working than other indentured servants. The tannery owner hired him to spy on his son, who kept the company of "a disreputable lot of medical men who shared his unwholesome interest in the dissection of cadavers" (114). The butchery that is the main recurrent image in the book has a submotif in the actions of these vivisectionists (or "resurrectionists," as they call themselves). Stubbs tells gruesome and occasionally hilarious stories of how he would have to dress in women's clothing to attend births as the practice of these resurrectionists led them into a strange underworld. But the tales gradually reveal the racism of his fellow resurrectionists, who endeavor to demonstrate the differences between races by examining anatomy and who put a high price on a particular specimen: a black female cadaver who was pregnant at the time of death.

Stubbs develops a grudging respect for the tannery owner's son because of his obsession with carefully capturing his world in drawings and because he turned his interest in anatomy into an art. The role of the artist—obsessive, monkish, slightly out of touch with mainstream society—becomes the point of Stubbs's story. Like many of the subjects of Wideman's stories, he is left with a desire so strong it is nearly an insatiable hunger for "what was next and next and next" (126). This desire is thwarted in the New World because of the madness of slavery: "The madness driving men to trade in human flesh, buying and selling one another like wood, or cattle. How could I be an artist in a land prospering from such commerce" (127). The question is not only Liam's, but Wideman's as well. The obsessive art of examining the depth of things—of cutting beneath the surface to expose the truth—is after all what Wideman does, but Liam suffers a crisis of faith about whether such meticulous rendering will do the world any good, or will provide a cure for what ails humankind.

Liam's other crisis is that he never managed to have children with Mrs. Stubbs. This confession is one that undergirds the other crises in the novel and leads The Reverend back into a dream about the prophecy of the cattle killing. He awakens to find that the Stubbs couple's house is on fire and learns that the townspeople have burned it during a night of rape, murder, and destruction. The images run together, in typical Wideman fashion, without revealing a clear picture of reality; however, the pattern of plague, disrupted lineage, and racial violence is clear enough, and this pattern is the key to understanding both the past and the present.

The second half of the book announces the theme of the dangers of false prophecy explicitly in its epigraph. The prophecy of the cattle killing leads to nothing more than self-destruction, like the image of the woman drowning herself carrying the futile figure of an already dead child. The survival of a people depends upon the truth that is passed down in stories from one generation to another, as the first sentence indicates: "Just as I sit beside you on this bed, speaking to you, the dead speak to me" (153). In the second section of the novel, Wideman blends fact and fiction using a variety of modes (such as letters), consistent with the earliest works of the English fictional tradition that were developed around the time of the novel's main setting. The initial story is of Absalom Jones and Richard Allen, who were driven out of the white church and went on to found a separate black church that became A.M.E. (founded in

Philadelphia in the early nineteenth century). As the second half of the novel includes more historical facts, it becomes clear that Wideman has chosen to set his complex tale at a point in history when democracy, scientific exploration, and religious reform led to the beginning of the United States, but also to point out how excluded and subjugated black people were during these processes. In the first letter of part 2, for instance, the author speaks of a balloon launched from the Walnut Street jail in Philadelphia in 1793 and extols the fact that a black servant accompanied the white pilot on this voyage: "whose blood better than the Negroes', with its tropical lushness and excitability, to record the heart's fluctuations as the balloon rose" (160). The passage recalls the exploits of the resurrectionists from the first section, whose assumptions about black bodies caused white people to treat black people as commodities even in death.

Immediately after the Philadelphia epidemic, some members of the white community turn against the black community, blaming them for importing the plague but also denigrating them for charging exorbitant rates for attending to the afflicted during the plague. These charges are yet another excuse for segregating and ultimately destroying the black community, just as the Stubbs house was eventually burned in the first section. It is left to one Doctor Benjamin Thrush—whose name ironically connotes an infectious disease—to mediate the racial controversy circulating in an inflammatory pamphlet. It is his wife who writes many of the substantial letters that make up the narrative, and she is also the unnamed ailing woman from part 1 who listens to The Reverend's stories. Her letters come together to form a book, consistent with the epistolary style of many eighteenth-century novels; yet it is a tame, well-meaning book in which "gentle readers" are "invited to spy on the intimate doings of their betters and also permitted to disclaim any immoral or prurient interest in such spying, since after all, what's being read is mere make-believe, a novel" (183). This art form is in direct contrast with the furiously imaginative painting of Liam Stubbs—"Always unknown. Always free" (182)—even if not a direct representation of reality. There is a parallel between these artistic styles and the methods of reform black and white people undertake to rebuild in the aftermath of the plague. Mrs. Thrush's well-meaning efforts to fund a black orphanage, for instance, just breed resentment on the part of the orphans, whose descriptions of their circumstances are reminiscent of the Middle Passage of slavery. The orphans perish in yet another fire, and The Reverend—whose identity melds with Wideman's as the novel travels across time—loses his faith not only in religion and social reform but also in stories: "The stories are not working" (205). He begins to stutter under the weight of so many dead, of so many stories of the suffering of Africans and their descendants. And yet he goes on telling stories, "one story never quite erased by the next, each story saving the space, saving itself, saving us" (208). In a final postmodern gesture, Wideman concludes with his own son Dan reading *The Cattle Killing* and commenting on it as a mysterious book, "full of silence and pain at the core" (209). Dan actually discovered some eighteenth-century letters by Africans in the British Museum and offers one as the fitting conclusion of this book. The letter emphasizes the idea that the Africans aided in their own destruction by following the false prophecy and holds out hope that their people can transcend this historical moment.

Wideman's next novel, *Two Cities* (1998), shares this theme to some degree, but it does so without the same level of experimentation with form. The novel's chapters are titled, blurring the boundaries between genres in typical Wideman fashion as the reader wonders initially whether these are interrelated stories. Billed as "A Love Story" on the dust jacket, it is a tale of how love can be a healing force after tragedy and loss. Wideman also revisits the role of the artist in the figure of Martin Mallory and continues his inquiry into the fate of MOVE by introducing its founder John Africa as a character. But the main story line is the romantic encounter between Kassima and Robert, both of whom borrow elements from Wideman's personal story.

The first chapter introduces the idea behind the "two cities" of the title. Literally they are Pittsburgh and Philadelphia—the two main cities of Wideman's writing—but figuratively they connote the motion between two worlds, which could be the past or the present, or the divide between life and death. The novel opens with Mr. Mallory reminiscing about his friend John Africa (who died in the attack on the MOVE compound) and wishing he were still alive to provide answers to the basic questions of existence and the thorny questions about why the police bombed the compound. The two cities and Mallory's relationship with John Africa are developed in two later chapters in the novel entitled "Philadelphia" and "Pittsburgh." When he lived in Philadelphia, Mallory had developed a friendship with John Africa, known as "the Dogman" because he walked dogs for pay.

Mallory is a photographer (though he claims he is "not an artist" [81]), and he writes letters to the modern Italian sculptor Alberto Giacometti, claiming not to know whether the famous artist is alive or dead. Through Mallory's one-sided conversation, Wideman reveals a good deal about his own art. One crucial concept is that "artists can't copy what they see. . . . They copy their memories" (82). Like Wideman, who privileges consciousness over realism, Mallory resolves to "stop asking [his] pictures to be mirrors" and admit that they are "memories, wishes, dreams" (82). The artist does not describe the world as it is but rather how he perceives it. The world changes, and the artist finds it impossible to freeze a moment in a world in flux. This conversation goes a long way toward explaining Wideman's near obsession with memory and his need to revisit moments from his past repeatedly. Mallory's chapter—the longest in the book—takes place right after Kassima has announced his death, reinforcing the novel's concerns with memory and the way it blurs the border between life and afterlife. Mallory does not seem to care whether or not Giacometti is alive or dead, just that he has learned a valuable aesthetic lesson from him: to create art with many layers that "will remind people to keep a world alive around them, to keep themselves alive at the center of a storm of swirling emptiness" (91). This pronouncement explains the author's aesthetic while nodding to his fascination with survival in a world that lacks inherent meaning.

If Mallory's story is about the way art and life interact, the other main plot involving Kassima and Robert is about how love can sustain two people who have suffered. Perpetuating the motif of the vital importance of memory, Robert grew up in a house very much like Kassima's—perhaps even the same house—and his first tryst with her is laden with his memories of his childhood. Robert's journeys into his memory highlight the impermanence of people and places and emphasize the sense of decay and dissolution he feels in his own life. All depictions of the present weighed against the past depict a world in decline. The most poignant illustration of this idea is on the basketball court when Robert and some of the old guard play against a group of young kids. When Robert tries to claim he was fouled, one of the young kids pulls out a gun and fires two shots, the second one puncturing and deflating the basketball.

At first the relationship between Robert and Kassima is pure and tender. They need each other to dispel the sorrow in their lives, and the first day they spend together lodges in Robert's memory as the best of his life. At the end of the chapter "Dancing at Edgar's," he intimates that he lost her and compares this loss to the familiar image of a fisherman describing the one that got away, his hands growing bigger each time: "The guy's not lying. He feels the empty between his hands growing each time he tells his story" (47). Kassima for her part had been looking for just a one-night stand after being brought low by the deaths of her two sons (through gun violence) and ex-husband, who contracted AIDS in prison, all of which happened in the space of a year. She despairs of the state of black boys who "are born beating they hard heads against a brick wall" (55) and seeks comfort in the Bible. She believes that Robert is different from other black men, but is sadly disappointed when she realizes that he is like others who "always got to prove something" (61). When Robert has the altercation on the basketball court, she both declares her love for him and tells him that she cannot be with him: "I've loved my last dead man" (76). He cannot accept that their relationship is over so abruptly, but she is resolute and does not contact him until she really needs him—when her tenant and friend Mr. Mallory dies.

Mallory's art has a social purpose as well as a philosophical intent. The one time Robert actually saw Mallory was in a post office when a pair of young gang members had set the other customers on edge. Mallory approached them with his camera, asking only whether he could take their picture, but he followed up this request by questioning them about why they did not rush to help when police were attacking the MOVE compound. Again, the parallels to Wideman are evident: the artist tries to make a difference, but someone with a gun is more in control of reality. The sentiment about weapons applies both to the police in their actions toward MOVE and to his own brother and son, imprisoned because of murderous violence. In another parallel, Mallory is wracked with guilt for leaving his wife and children, echoing Wideman's divorce at the time the novel was published. Finally, Mallory is conscious of the way his art tends to separate him from others; in another letter to Giacometti, he writes, "What is the language of your art. Did you ever feel it was hated, a language that tainted you, cut you off from others, mocked you, mocked your efforts to share mind and heart" (128).

Mallory's death brings Robert and Kassima back together, but it also provides a new burden for them. Mallory had crawled naked into Kassima's bed before dying, and Robert at first feels anger at what he interprets as an invasion of his territory. But this emotion quickly turns to pity and even empathy as he realizes that death is everyone's fate. Kassima confesses that she had been wanting to get back together with Robert and that she had hoped Mallory would have been the key factor in their reunion, but her true dilemma is that Mallory had asked her to burn his photos after he dies, something she does not want to do. Her inner dilemma is that she wants to be self-reliant and tough but also that she wants to make herself vulnerable enough so that she can love.

Two Cities continues to traverse time and space as the novel journeys between Philadelphia, Pittsburgh, and beyond. Mallory recalls his time as a soldier in Italy, how he and a colleague named Gus, after a tryst with two Italian girls, woke up to dodge the rain of bullets all around them. Gus died in the firefight and Mallory was left to piece together his memories of that event, which run together with the attack on the MOVE compound and also a gunfight in a diner in Philadelphia: "Same dying. Same lies to cover it up. Same clean slate. So true it's past true, past time, place, and color" (197). The novel's concerns with violence and incarceration swirl together in Mallory's head. His only recourse is to cultivate his art, which is an attempt to capture the invisible truths around him, the sorrow that underpins his reality and causes him to sing his own version of the blues.

Kassima has no creative outlet such as photography to rescue her from the despair of her difficult life. Mallory had praised her for avoiding bitterness, but she lives in fear that bitterness is her fate. Mallory believes he should be considered the best blues singer in the world, but his singing is entirely internal: he keeps his blues voice confined to his head, "where it's perfect" (217). But art, if it is to do any social good, must have an audience. Mallory's funeral is held at the same time as a murdered gang member's, and the funeral parlor erupts in mayhem. Kassima is desperate to retrieve the photographs that Mallory left behind, which are in the funeral parlor ready to be cremated along with his body. John Africa had in fact told Mallory about the dangers of keeping ideas and expressions locked inside of the mind: the philosophy of MOVE is to make the invisible visible, to display the war that is raging silently in contemporary society. The novel's final scene is richly symbolic: Mallory's coffin is desecrated in the melee at the funeral home, and Kassima is moved to distribute his photographs while excoriating the gang members who are enacting this senseless violence.

Two Cities, like all the novels of Wideman's middle period, is a tour de force that engages his signature concerns: memory, art, storytelling, urban decay, and incarceration. There is something hopeful as this love story might result in a lasting relationship between Robert and Kassima (who is pregnant at the end) or at least show that there is new life after so much death. The novel showcases an attempt to reconcile some fundamental opposites—male and female, young and old—that have been at odds in Wideman's work throughout his career, and yet the fundamental social power dynamics are a cause of despair, as those with power continuously oppress those without power. The role of the artist in relation to this dynamic is always a difficult one to define, but Wideman's attempts to do so are especially poignant in these works.

CHAPTER 6

Creolizing Genres

Wideman has never been easily characterized in terms of genre. Many of his works are hybrids of fictional and nonfictional forms (what Byerman called "Wideman's Mash-Ups").[1] As discussed earlier, he has become less content to stick to a particular genre as his career has progressed, allowing his nonfictional personae to enter freely into fictional spaces and exit without notice or apology. This impulse is partly resistance to existing forms that can be constraining and partly invention as he comes to develop not only a unique style but a unique form as well. The reader of Wideman's late works must be willing to revise or abandon preconceived notions of genre. Four of these works in particular—*Hoop Roots,* (2001), *The Island: Martinique* (2003), *Fanon* (2008), and *Writing to Save a Life* (2016)—best represent his tendency late in his career to produce books that resist categorization. Evident in these works and in many of his later stories discussed in chapter 7 is an obsession with death and a quest for heroes.

Hoop Roots is the most fully realized of these late works and should be counted among Wideman's best works. At times uncomfortably frank, at times lyrically beautiful, it is a unique work that shows and extends the range of Wideman's capabilities intellectually, emotionally, and aesthetically. Its ostensible subject—playground basketball—is a fitting vehicle for Wideman's broader mediations on writing, race, his own story, Homewood, contemporary American culture, and oral tradition, in addition to a host of other topics. He arrives at the realization that individuals grow, grow old, and die, prompting a quest for cultural expressions that endure. Playground hoop is a portal to the stories that Wideman tells, stories that would otherwise die out, taking with them a vital part of African American culture. It is a book about resurrection, survival, and refusing the appearance of death's permanence. He declares it an homage to W. E. B. DuBois's *The Souls of Black Folk,* which he describes as "model, guide, beacon," and its dedication to his lover Catherine Nedonchelle, whom he would later marry, marks a decided break in his personal story. In the opening paragraphs of the first chapter, "More," he meditates on his aging body and on the fact that his children are grown, and he admits, "my marriage of thirty-plus years has unraveled" (3), making *Hoop Roots* a necessary catharsis for him; he is "starting a story so a story can end" (3). He is marking his shift into a new phase of his life, in other words, one in which playground basketball is now something he is more likely to watch than to participate in. The recurrent point he makes, though, is that basketball continues even as players grow old and die. The game itself is a way of collapsing past, present, and future into the African concept of Great Time in which all occur simultaneously. Thus he can blend memory and desire and fuse them into a unique work. He begins the book by declaring it "no book" (3), destabilizing the project immediately so that the casual reader who thinks he or she has picked up a book about basketball will know immediately that this is something different: not exactly about basketball and not even a book.

Of course, it *is* about basketball in a profound way, but basketball serves as metaphor or analogy for a host of other subjects. The game was Wideman's salvation when he was young and in search of a masculine bonding experience as the oldest son in a family of matriarchs with a largely absent father. It was also, like writing, a vehicle for his unique talents, and he gets a good deal of mileage out of the parallels between the two activities. Both allow him to examine his multiple selves. Both either accommodate or resist a main "spine of action" (10), the "story line" of narratives that Wideman frequently manipulates. Indeed, in the table of contents for this volume, he invites the reader to "read [the chapters] in sequence, or improvise." The "more" of the title of the first chapter stems from an insatiable desire he derives from playground basketball—a game that never truly ends—and translates directly to writing: "Seeking more means self-discovery. Means redefining the art I practice. In the present instance, wanting to compose and share a piece of writing that won't fail because it might not fit someone else's notion of what a book should be" (13). This declaration of artistic autonomy is immediately compromised by a sense, related to DuBois's notion of double-consciousness, that his work will be judged by the rigid standards of white literature: "One of the worst trials for Americans of visible African descent . . . is the perpetual fear of not measuring up to standards established by so-called white people who imagine themselves the standard issue and also presume themselves to be the issuers of standards" (13). To shake this fear, he writes a book that is "no book" and creates a unique form that is a hybrid of autobiography, philosophy, parable, confession, and history.

"More" is an impressive, densely packed memoir that serves as a good inroad into Wideman's late-career work and might even serve as a fitting introduction to his overall oeuvre. He connects three of his main interests—music, the stories of his family, and basketball—in such a way as to frame his main concerns, which are all held together by that desire for more, a concept he has raised repeatedly throughout his career as the driving force in his life. The desire for more, he suggests, was a stumbling block to some of his Homewood peers who did not know what to do with it. For him, it was a catalyst into the wider world, albeit one that caused him the type of anxiety he has wrestled with throughout his career: bluntly, what did he sacrifice as he left behind his family and neighborhood? What did he gain? The memoir frames a story that his grandfather told him about finding a gold piece between the logs of the meager cabin where he grew up. His fantasies about what to do with the money gave way to suspicions that no one would believe he simply found it. He assumed it was placed there by one of his ancestors during slavery, something precious squirreled away so that a young person such as himself might find it in better times. And yet he hid it again, where it remains to this day, useless. It is an anecdote about what one does with the valuable things one discovers. Without stating the moral explicitly, Wideman retells it as a way to justify his own drive, the lesson he learned from music and basketball: "Music said there's much more to life than meets the eye and said you were born with a gift, a faculty something like an eye or ear, and if you learn how to make it pay attention, it will reveal much more about the more there is to life, the more there is to you" (16). This gift is his writing, and it makes his experience richer and marks his difference from others, a difference about which he feels ambivalent.

The second memoir in the collection, "My First Shot," focuses on the intersection of gender and racial identity. Wideman looks for the origins of his fascination with the game and constructs some possible stories around the first time he ever shot a basketball. He remembers the very spot where it happened, on the precise dividing line between black and white people on the edge of Homewood. White men would gather to shoot hoops during their lunch break from a factory, and in watching them Wideman realized he was breaking the rules set by the women in his family, but he realizes as an adult that they knew he would: "How else keep alive in their male children the cute, mischievous twinkle racial oppression strives to extinguish" (27). Though as a child he imagines the women watching his every move, he now realizes they were preoccupied with real trouble, especially his mother, who was trying to cope with the absence of his father after the couple split up. The details of his first shot do not matter; the way he constructs the story as a platform for meditation on broader issues is what is truly important.

"My First Shot" ranges broadly, returning to the basketball court as a sacred space within a crumbling world. It is where masculine codes are passed between generations. He concentrates on a man named Ed Fleming, a member of the generation before his who taught Wideman a few hard lessons on the court, the same lessons John's absent father once taught Ed. He meets Ed after many years in a funeral home: Wideman's nephew Omar has been killed in a turf war. (Omar was Robby's son, a fact that reiterates the pattern of absent fathers and street crime.) This circumstance causes him to worry about the rise of gang violence in his old neighborhood and the implications for the loss of culture transmitted on the basketball court. The lessons of the court are essential, just as they are in jazz music, but both require a sensitive ear: "You can pick up in the playing if you listen hard, listen easy enough, the chorus saying, We are doing this together and it's just us out here but the game has been here before, other players have found themselves in the middle of this same deep, good shit and figured out how to deal" (49). Playground basketball is about survival, but it is also an art, a connection to the past, a testing ground for heroes, a seedbed for stories, and a free space where oppressed men can exercise their autonomy. He compares Ed Fleming to the NBA superstar Michael Jordan and ends up elevating Ed as the kind of hero who has long been unsung but remains pure in the absence of the taint of commercialism.

"Learning to Play" is the longest and most complex piece in *Hoop Roots* and also the one that has the least to do with playground basketball, despite the fact that it contains a passage that explains the unspoken rules of the court for the benefit of those who have not spent a lifetime trying to interpret them. Aside from basketball, its main subjects are the death of his grandmother when he was a teen, the guilty connection between her death and Wideman's budding sexual desire for women, and the way his relationships with women have begun and ended. Under the surface, the memoir works through the difficulty of reconciling multiple selves.

"Learning to Play" contains some of Wideman's rawest confessions. As a teen, he volunteers to return to the Homewood of his youth after his mother has moved to the white neighborhood of Shadyside. His role in Homewood is ostensibly to watch his convalescent grandmother, but he escapes for hours each day to play basketball. He acknowledges the complex structure of the piece and draws an analogy between his digressions and basketball itself: "I'm in too many places at once. On the court playing ball before I finish what I started—confessing, telling the story of a boy and his grandmother. Hoop a big part of it, obviously, but hoop also a way of breaking up the story, escaping then and ever since" (111). His guilt is multilayered. He projects desire onto his grandmother's withered body, then admits that he nearly wished for her death so that his desires could attach themselves to a young woman. There is a photo of him as a baby grabbing his grandmother's braid: "a roly-poly baby with his handful of hair who maybe hasn't been half as happy since" (72). This is a profound revelation of his damaged psyche, and in fact "Learning to Play" is one of the most concentrated, sustained looks we have of the Wideman's tormented mind. He speaks at many turns, from the first paragraph on, of how he is made up of many selves, some of which are alien to his conscious mind.

He gradually reveals that his unhappiness has its roots in this summer with his grandmother that coincided with his parents' separation. The theme again is that he was growing into masculine maturity with no role models. The memoir was written soon after the dissolution of his own marriage of more than thirty years and framed by scenes from a short-lived affair with a woman he had met in Philadelphia three decades earlier. (He refers to her as his "rebound" relationship, consistent with the basketball conceit that controls the book). Perhaps because the guiding lesson from the court was competition, he reveals how this relationship was tainted by his insistence that he and his lover tell stories of their sexual pasts, which turns into a competition that alienates them from one another: omitting the question mark (which becomes a cornerstone of his late style) he asks her, "Doesn't the best story win " (123). But he also distorts her story, viewing it through the lens of racial oppression even though that had not been her intent. He admits his ambivalence: "I don't want it to be about race. . . . I'd feel great if I could forgive and forget. But I can't. Not yet. Not while they're still chopping us down and trying to stomp life out of the pieces" (122). The I/they dichotomy is complicated by the fact that this lover is black, while his long-term relationships are with white women, and he is of mixed ancestry, as was his maternal grandmother, whom the story is largely about. Staring at her intently when he was a child, he realizes "her skin wasn't one color but many, paleness dotted and speckled with darker bits of various hues" (75). The difficulty of love, which is certainly a core theme of this memoir, is intensified by race relations. The more he examines the room where he watched his grandmother—a psychological space from which he cannot escape, even as an adult—the deeper he is able to explore his mind, which harbors the scars not only of his personal history, but of the vexed history of his people.

Having drifted far from basketball in "Learning to Play," he refocuses on the sport in the next two pieces. He subtitles "Who Invented the Jump Shot" a "fable," and it does share qualities with the fabulous: free invention departing from strict fact to produce a tale with a moral, but not one that is clear to everyone. It is framed by Wideman himself, who is about to speak on the topic that gives the piece its title at an academic popular culture conference. As when he traded erotic stories with his lover in "Learning to Play," his mind-set is deeply affected by race relations. His mind travels to a scene from 1927 in which the newly formed Harlem Globetrotters basketball team traveled across snowy landscapes to play an exhibition game in Illinois. There was one white man in the car—the driver and team's manager—and Wideman's consciousness touches down in his mind. The car's interior is a recurrent setting throughout the piece, but Wideman's imagination is able to roam over time and space to spin out the fable that does everything but answer the question "Who invented the jump shot?" What it does instead is examine the forces behind the question: the appropriation of black culture by white people, white people's anxious and sometimes violent responses to perceived threats from the black community, and the repetition of historical patterns that keep power structures intact. In the story's frame tale, Wideman initially comes across as almost paranoid, but the fable's free-flowing form enables him to escape paranoia and produce a thought-provoking story that has less to do with the author's experience than with his capacity for invention.

If "Who Invented the Jump Shot" is pure invention, it has its counterpart in the next piece, "The Village," which is more cultural analysis than story or memoir. Its analysis complements the other pieces by using basketball as a jumping-off point to delve deep into history. He validates it as a form of folk art, parallel to storytelling, music, dance, and similar expressions, like the African beading custom that provides the epigraph for many of the book's chapters; he writes about how he is attempting "to demonstrate how sport is art and, like any other African-American art form, expresses and preserves, if you teach yourself how to look, the deep structure, both physical (material) and metaphysical (immaterial), of a culture" (185). Although there is an autobiographical element to the story—he and his lover, Catherine, pause to watch a playground game while waiting for a movie to start—he is largely removed from this piece, using an anthropologist's lens. He manages to connect basketball to the Carnival tradition in Caribbean cultures, to the history of minstrelsy, and to street hustles such as shining shoes and three-card Monte. He "reads" certain fashion styles on the court (such as the length of basketball shorts) and styles of play, connecting them to the crass commercialism of the NBA weighed against the democratic, locally controlled parameters of the playground game. Part of his role is to interpret what he sees for the benefit of his white, female counterpart (and also for the reader), but he pulls up short toward the end when he recognizes that his denigration of a flashy player on the court might be related to his jealousy of the boy, who is young, brash, and still in the process of figuring out the grim truths that weigh on Wideman's psyche.

But the game, he says in many places throughout the book, is about experience, about actually playing rather than anything abstract. This is why in "Naming the Court" he chooses to honor the playground legends of the past who would otherwise go unnoticed and unrecorded. The park in Homewood where he learned to play was named Westinghouse Park after a white inventor-industrialist. Wideman argues passionately that it should be named instead after one of two Homewood heroes. The first is Maurice Stokes, a role model for Wideman, who rose up to play professionally for one season only to be taken down by an injury that rendered him immobile and eventually killed him. The other is even less likely: Eldon Lawson, who is now in prison with Wideman's brother Robby and who never accomplished anything noteworthy in the traditional sense of the word. But much of Wideman's project in *Hoop Roots* is to reframe the discussion of what we value culturally as a way of validating the achievements of black men who lived and suffered, who struggled against their prescribed fate against all odds. He acknowledges the suffering: "Some names leak glory, but often names also leak tears, especially when the names are drawn from the history of African peoples in the New World. *Malcolm*. Tears and more tears till the ground beneath our feet is as wet and slippery as those cobbled alleys behind slaughterhouses in colonial Philadelphia" (195). He alludes to a history of atrocities leading up to the current incarceration crisis in the African American community, explicitly naming his brother and son as its victims. The weight of this analysis intensifies his desire to rename the basketball court named for a white inventor in a black neighborhood. He writes, "I'm not suggesting we should return the park or the nation to sender. Even if the idea appeals to me, there's no place, no way really to send them, except up in smoke, and we've tried that before, in the sixties, and found fire's often satisfying but no solution" (199). The act of renaming the park is not only less destructive but more in keeping with the spirit of the book, which is a celebration of African American expressions that resist mainstream white culture and thus uphold a sense of community, even if it is one not recognized as such.

Despite the depth of layering and range of subjects in *Hoop Roots,* Wideman manages to tie together all the book's major concerns in the final piece, "One More Time." It takes the form of a letter to his grandmother Freeda French, picking up where he left off in "Learning to Play" by explaining to her his complex feelings during the summer he spent with her as she approached death. In the course of the letter he alludes to scenes from all the other pieces in the book. He pauses at length on a photo of Freeda when she was a young mother, and his analysis of it mirrors the work he has been doing throughout *Hoop Roots:* to see the complexity in a piece of art someone might take for granted, such as a photograph, a game of basketball, a dance, or a blues lyric.

He concludes, "A culture's art shouts and whispers secrets the culture couldn't exist without, unveils its reason for being" (230). In the case of African Americans, he believes that African cultures "are still vibrant in us, if we teach ourselves how to look and listen, how to speak their primal, engendering languages that discipline desire" (230). In many ways Wideman has been instructing the reader "how to look and listen" throughout the book and arguably throughout his career. The stories of society's outcasts or invisible citizens are like games of playground basketball: easily overlooked but culturally vital. He compares basketball to the ancient tradition of the "ring shout," a sacred ritual that unites the living and the dead, the seen and the unseen, and the past, present, and future. His letter to his grandmother at the end of this collection performs the same function.

Ultimately *Hoop Roots* is among the more optimistic works Wideman has written. Like *Brothers and Keepers,* it is a celebration of the spirit in a world threatened by materialistic values. Contemporary reviewers offered a mixture of opinions. Will Blythe in the *New York Times* called it uneven, faulting its erudite passages for resembling "a contest played by graduate students in critical theory."[2] Renee Graham in the *Boston Globe* was much more laudatory, calling it "poignant" and praising Wideman's "jazz-riff ruminations on race and American Society"[3] as much as meditations on basketball. In a more recent appraisal, Karen Jahn claimed that in *Hoop Roots* "Wideman becomes a jazz artist . . . [improvising] on representative black male twentieth-century experiences, making them his own."[4]

There is a crossover from *Hoop Roots* to *The Island: Martinique* at a moment when Wideman analyzes basketball as a parallel to Carnival and other expressions of folk culture: "Playground hoop, like the Creole of Martinique, for instance, is a self-sufficient language. Speakers of Creole don't practice their vernacular in order to become better speakers of the island's official French dialect. Creole speakers aren't aspiring to 'whiteness'" (*Hoop Roots*, 174). The books, published just two years apart, have much in common, including their hybrid forms, both of which contain fables, autobiography, history, and cultural analysis. *The Island: Martinique* is a book whose threefold purpose is destabilization, displacement, and invention. Even the first sentence of the book, even the first word, is destabilizing: "Here I am on the brink of returning to Martinique, still trying to make sense of my first and only trip to the island" (xix). The word "here" of course signifies place, and the book is titled after a specific and self-bounded place, yet the "here" that is the first word of the book refers either to a temporal or psychological moment, rather than to a physical place. Where is Wideman as he writes that line, on what kind of "brink," and where is the reader in relation to him?

The typical travel memoir is written for the benefit of an audience who knows less about a place than the author does. Again, however, Wideman destabilizes this expectation by denying his role as expert, as he has only made a single trip to the island, one that is paradoxically his "first and only." In the second paragraph he reveals that he is on a very different island—Manhattan—and his only physical connection to Martinique is the most trivial version of travel literature imaginable: "souvenir place mats with picture-perfect splashes of Martinique" (xix). His attempts to research the place are thwarted: "[I] intended to steep myself in everything I could learn about it before I returned. Strangely, the information I've been able to absorb . . . has operated to distance as much as familiarize" (xx). The reader who has picked up this travel memoir as a guidebook is clearly in for a surprise as the author both denies his own authority and suggests that the island is inscrutable, if not unknowable. He describes his assignment as "the opportunity to go anywhere in the world and write about it" (xx). He decides to "attempt Martinique" more or less arbitrarily and expresses a desire to be taught by his subject. He announces his rhetorical intent explicitly: "That readers might also be engaged, pushed, entertained and instructed by my rendering of a subject is an outcome I desire, but finally do not control" (xxi). Such a conclusion puts a burden on the reader, and yet the verbs Wideman chooses are expressed in the passive voice: to *be* engaged and pushed (not to mention the more familiar verbs associated with reading literature, "entertained" and "instructed") requires a certain commitment and willingness on the part of the reader who may be resistant if other travel literature is the model, for the reader of the guidebook is perhaps the most passive reader imaginable, one who explicitly demands, "Tell me what to do when I go somewhere unfamiliar."

Finally, Wideman articulates his perspective in his introduction, which blends with that of Catherine, his companion, who is French. The two of them together constitute what Wideman calls "a kind of insider/outsider status" based on their language—Catherine's perfect French and Wideman's knowledge of "Afro-American vernaculars [he had] grown up speaking" (xxi), which will provide him with a key to understanding the Creole of Martinique—but also race, as she is white. Speaking of the island's "mix of African and European elements" (xxi), he alludes to African American history but also recognizes in the island "the sort of clarifying distance and difference I desired, especially since it's so difficult to achieve at home in the States" (xxi). He is "at home in the States" while penning these words, indicating the radical displacement that his inquiry into Martinique yields. Americans do not typically refer to their nation as "the States" except while abroad. Wideman has projected himself into a new psychological space while writing, a new imagined territory that will open up the space for his nonliteral and nonlinear exploration of Martinique.

The remainder of Wideman's introduction continues to problematize the travel genre and his role in contributing to it. As Guzzio wryly noted, "One wonders if this is what National Geographic had in mind"[5] when they commissioned the book. Wideman addresses the reader at one point with a kind of challenge: "I hope I'm providing an incentive for your journey to Martinique, and helping you imagine what might be at stake when you go" (xxiii). He also admits that there are "plenty better places to steep yourself in Martinican facts, lore, stats" (xxiv) than this book provides. What, then, do we have here? Not a guide book, nor a history, but, in his words, "the record, written and rewritten, of a visit—a single visit, one visit to check out the island firsthand—and various acts of return: homage, meditation, analysis, fiction, imagining, *déjà vu*, mourning" (xxiv). The words "fiction" and "imagining" at the center of this litany signal, again, a triangulation, this time of the experiential and the informative. There is the island Wideman found, the island the reader expects to encounter, and finally an island that is a shared landscape, created as much as discovered.

The genre of *The Island: Martinique* would be difficult to describe in any way other than as a varied list, with no one item outweighing the others or occupying a central position. Such lists are in fact a common and consistent feature throughout the book. For example, Wideman describes Martinican radical Frantz Fanon in the following terms: "Fanon's performance is often pure Creole in its irony, wit, bricolage, anger, mimicry, wisdom, brutal honesty, its ambivalence toward authority" (48). Wideman models his own aesthetic after Fanon's "pure Creole" performance and goes on to define creolization further, which again helps define this book: "Creolization means taking nothing for granted. In the case of Martinique, it means not accepting the authority of French (the island's official language). Creolization works like elegy—lyrically summoning what's absent and desired. It is skeptical, it peers into cracks, despises easy answers, attacks language, undermines, revitalizes, reroutes, personalizes words" (48). All of these qualities are also true of Wideman's approach to travel writing. *The Island: Martinique* might most accurately be described as a creolized approach to travel literature, history, and fiction, but even that definition is only an approximation. According to Gerald Bergevin, "*The Island* contributes to Wideman's career-long project to reconstruct the historical record while simultaneously providing a personal testimony of survival and renewal."[6]

Wideman structures the book in four parts with the fourth deliberately connecting with the first in a circle. There are recognizable patterns throughout: a tendency to see the ghosts of slavery and colonization at every turn, an obsession with economic power, and a raw engagement with the turbulence of love. The first section, "Journal," by far the longest, is an intellectual tour de force but lacks a central narrative arc. The reader of this section is likely to feel more like an intruder than a tourist. Wideman opens the door wide into his own difficulties—the love affair following a painful divorce, the disappointment he and his lover feel to learn she is not pregnant, the admission that he did not feel overwhelming and immediate love when they first became involved, his troubled dreams in which he imagines himself enslaved, and so forth. Its tendency is toward confession and analysis more than surface observation, and yet he continually returns his gaze to Martinique for inspiration.

In the journal, the island becomes overdetermined: John and Katrine (as she is called in this section) might each separately be the island, or they might together constitute it. They are also Columbus landing on the island or other vague explorers sailing toward it as "paradise" (22), a figment of their imaginations, but at the same time the physical island is the reality to which they return. Wideman compares Katrine's womb to Port Royal, Martinique's old capital, under siege in a historical battle after they accept that there is no baby. The reader encounters the actual Martinique with John and Katrine but never simply to visit, always to analyze. Touring a cemetery, John expresses the desire to mingle with the visitors and mourners who congregate there, but, he says, "I don't want to appear like a tourist. Obnoxious, intrusive, an unconnected outsider, temporary, phony, demanding, superior, irrelevant like a tourist." Katrine asks, "what's wrong with being a tourist anyway. Can't people be tourists without being assholes" (26). John lets the question hang, unanswered, but later takes up tourism as a "useful metaphor for anybody's sojourn here on earth" (26–27).

It should be clear that the journal section and the book more generally are as far away as possible from the bullet-pointed suggestions in travel articles that begin, "If you go. . . ." Wideman's musings are more along the lines of "Why do you go?" or "Why go anywhere?" or even "Why are we here?" This journal, which takes up roughly two-thirds of the book, is reminiscent of Thoreau's *Walden*. Martinique is less a place, in this sense, than a space for reflection. At the same time, the specific history of Martinique, the ghosts of its troubled past, continually present themselves to Wideman's imagination. Thoreau-like, Wideman penetrates the exterior of experience and repeatedly comes up with the difficult questions that have haunted Martinique ever since it was named as such: colonial conquest, enslavement, economic exploitation, and cultural suppression. Even the rare moments that seem like typical Caribbean fun in the sun are tainted: on a day when he deliberately takes a break to enjoy the physical beauty of the place, the delicious food and wine, the indulgence in sexual pleasure, Wideman is troubled by a visit to the Museum of the History of Cane, where he bitterly reflects on "the white, pure sweetener Europe was willing to pay for with its soul" (83). On this island that represents a clash of European desire and African subjugation, he finds himself reflecting on his own nation, describing himself and his countrymen "as united as the fingers of a hand in a fist when fists are necessary, and separate and different as those same fingers when it comes to what each receives as a fair share of bounties and privileges . . . equally inseparable, separately unequal, one big happy *us* against the world" (72). Largely concerned with the way the "new world" was a product of the European exploitation of African slave labor, he also implicates his own country, and even himself, in the process of economic exploitation that has created the contemporary Caribbean. This theme is evident in the Pere Labat story, section 2 of the book, in which the legendary figure is seen traveling from a port in Europe in the eighteenth century to a modern-day mall in Martinique, where he buys Nike sneakers. Colonization and enslavement of old become creation of markets in the new global economy.

Even writing about Martinique, Wideman admits, is a kind of colonization: "Writers can be the worst kind of colonizers, ruthlessly taking over and exploiting a place for their own purposes" (xxv). He later compares himself to Columbus and wonders whether all authors are "required by their trade to peek and pry, make presumptive strikes on other people's privacy" (29). His awareness of his complicity in the history of Martinique as a place shaped by colonial history creates a thick irony in a book that initially pretends to objectivity (with its map and list of dates) but quickly moves to an erasure of everything but the subjective: "Your Martinique is no more or less the Martinique than mine" (xxv). Martinique becomes a mystical dreamy template for the imagination, a place that is neither real nor imagined in any common definitions of those terms. In short, although *The Island: Martinique* seems initially to be motivated by exploration and encounter, it is actually motivated by invention; and Wideman makes an important move away from traditional postcolonial narratives, with their emphasis on binary power structures, to produce a new narrative that triangulates the Afro-Caribbean-American experience.

After the journal and legend of Pere Labat, the book veers into a work of fiction in which some experiences that were clearly those of John and Katrine in the journal are refigured in the characters Paul and Chantal before concluding with a nonfiction sketch that is one lengthy sentence. To describe the narrative as nonlinear, as Guzzio did, is an understatement, and yet Wideman's figure of circularity is not quite accurate either, for the return to the beginning is not a clean connection. The book's shape derives from a series of triangles inscribed within the circular figure: Europe/Africa/North America; recent past/historical past/present; black/white/brown; French/English/Creole. The book itself can be seen as a similarly triangulated genre that it shares with neo–slave narratives: journal/fiction/memoir. According to Guzzio, "There are tripartite structures of some form in all of Wideman's works," but he "seems to be experimenting with the number four in *The Island;* nonetheless, there are doubles in that work as well."[7] She is right, but perhaps geometry here is insufficient to describe this work, which unfolds and spills over in a decidedly nonmathematical way. Wideman's method is a deliberate flouting of genre itself, just as he flouts linguistic conventions throughout the text, such as omitting question marks after questions, dispensing with sentence structure in chapter 4 (which is made up of a single sentence, seventeen pages long), and placing epigraphs from Fanon throughout the story of Chantal and Paul rather than just at the beginning. The parallel between genre and his dominant thematic concerns is evident in the following quotation: "Is the only choice for Martinique either/or—French or West Indian. Why remain trapped within a racialized paradigm of essentialist oppositions—black or white, European or African. Must 'hybrids' be 'disembodied' and 'unsure.' Doesn't creolization embody the certainty of uncertainty and improvise rootedness with spontaneous performance" (97). We can add to this inquiry the question "Why does this book have to be labeled either fiction or travel literature?" Literary genre is not pure: its definition accrues and changes with its developments over time. In a cogent statement of his aesthetic beliefs, Wideman has said, "Art should always be something that to some degree shocks and changes people and worries people and contradicts what the king says. . . . That's its power, that's its joy. Play, illusion. Any constraints on that, any kind of rules or any allegiances that are externally imposed, have to be looked at by the artist with a lot of suspicion, a lot of skepticism."[8] His suspicious, skeptical response to the "rules" of genre, here and elsewhere, is to bend them to fit his purposes.

By approaching travel writing as an opportunity rather than a prescription, and by creolizing the various forms available to him, Wideman presents us with a text every bit as rich, mysterious, and difficult to describe as its subject, the island Martinique. In terms of how it functions as a variation on the neo–slave narrative genre, the most obvious points of entry are the journal section, in which he meditates at length on the island's history as a slave colony, and the Pere Labat story, in which the author's imagination transcends time to link the era of slavery with contemporary capitalism. It might be more productive, though, to focus on the book's final chapter, the lengthy sentence in which Wideman describes his and Katrine's visit to the ruins of St.-Pierre, a city destroyed by a volcano in 1902. Thirty thousand residents of St.-Pierre died in the catastrophe. Only two survived: a black man "confined drunk in a dungeon" and "a white man just extraordinarily lucky" (152). The free-flowing meditation occasioned by this visit is a concentrated example of what Wideman borrows from the neo–slave genre, and how he invents his unique response to it. Neo–slave works are about the persistence of historical trauma, the imperative of survival, and the haunting of history. As Wideman explores history's ruins, these dimensions of the genre impress his mind in a way that is intensely personal and coolly collective. Because Wideman is the author, the reader must delve below the surface of a challenging text to comprehend them.

The seventeen-page sentence is itself a journey across time and history, and it forces the reader to read attentively without the benefit of traditional structure and punctuation. The journey begins with the volcanic explosion and moves outward from that incident to cover most of the book's motifs: the strained, passionate relationship between John and Katrine, multiple phases of Martinique's history, Wideman's personal history, and the colonial project that unites all of these. His attention turns from the island's seventeenth-century mansion called Habitation Anse Latouche to the invisible labor that made it possible: "a vast, sulky posse of African slaves, fieldworkers who cultivate, cut, haul, and crush the cane, baptizing the land with their blood and sweat, African artisans and mechanics who built whatever the plantation required, African engineers, agronomists, wizards, musicians, whores, chroniclers, philosophers, mothers, scholars, drunks, cooks, runaways, saints, renegades, all colors, genders, ages, sizes invested here, imprisoned here, buried here, in this grave-quiet Habitation Latouche, Africans whose muteness, tonguelessness overcomes me, sits me down on a stone bench and keeps me sitting still" (160).

The narrative has consistently attempted to make visible the fact of suffering slaves or descendants of slaves who are invisible to the tourist vacationing in Martinique, even to those who take the time to explore ruins and sugar plantations instead of simply basking on beaches. What makes this passage so valuable is its revelatory power, not only to Wideman but also to the attentive reader. This "vast, sulky posse" is not unlike the title character in Morrison's *Beloved,* a ghost with a strong desire to communicate sorrow and suffering, and whose attempt to do so can only come through a troubling apparition.

The ghosts of slaves sit Wideman down on that stone bench for a specific purpose: "so I can listen, interrogate the silence with my own, attend the muted spirits, summon them, beg them to forgive me for appalling distance, appalling ignorance, forgive me for not avenging their terror, their captivity, their immolation" (161). At the heart of the neo–slave narrative is the compulsion to bear witness to history. Although Wideman has done so consistently throughout *The Island: Martinique* and throughout his career, there is something palpable and visceral about this particular encounter that intensifies its significance. Again, recalling Morrison's *Beloved* with its emphasis on sites of memory (124 Bluestone Road, the Clearing, Sweet Home), Wideman prepares himself to receive a particular message from the era of slavery in a particular place. The trappings of this encounter have religious overtones as he sits on a stone bench among stone ruins, and he and Katrine tacitly agree not to raise their voices above a whisper.

The voice from the past shatters the "thick, thick silence" that has descended upon them: "a sudden onslaught of howling startles us" (161). Although they had heard this noise before, Wideman cannot ascertain its origin, but one plausible explanation is that it comes from "the unquiet souls of those kidnaped and raped and tortured and worked to death on the island" (161). John and Katrine try to explain the sound rationally, ascribing it to peacocks, but they find no evidence of such birds and cannot find any information from a local girl because they cannot remember the word "peacock" in French: "so we left behind the silence, left behind as if they never happened the mysterious bawling, tortured screams" (163). However, Wideman does not leave these howls behind. They are, in fact, always in his mind, and they are part of the island, whose nickname he reveals in the book's very first paragraph: "*Le Pays des Revenants* . . . 'the country of comers-back'" (xix). "Ghosts" is a more common translation. The presence of these ghosts explains the author's persistent melancholy, as Bergevin has argued, and yet his awareness of the howling past of slavery is more than an occasion for mourning. It goes beyond even his own sense of helplessness and guilt, evident in his sorrowful message to his brethren "for not avenging their terror." Mourning, despair, and a rejection of material pleasures and comforts help constitute the substance of *The Island: Martinique,* but transcending all of these emotions is the urge to invent, to create new stories out of the ruins of the past. Wideman concludes his book in a state of excitement over "the need to tell," coupled with anxiety about his abilities: "nervous because I might screw it up, might leave out something real or intrude something fake and spoil it or might not remember to invent something when invention would render more life or might forget to prune facts when facts detract from vitality" (166). Despite this anxiety, he forges on and manages to find a way, through creolizing genres, to produce a unique literary work testifying to slavery's persistent effects.

Martinique is the birthplace of Frantz Fanon, the revolutionary author of *The Wretched of the Earth* and *Black Skin White Masks,* who was a foundational figure (along with Emmett Till) in the formation of Wideman's understanding of race from an early age. Wideman's most recent novel, *Fanon,* is an attempt to write Fanon's story in a way only Wideman could or would. It is labeled a novel on the book's jacket, but it is a hybrid genre just like *Hoop Roots* and *The Island: Martinique,* a bricolage of memoir, philosophical musings, fiction, biography, and fable. Halfway through the book, in a letter to Fanon himself, the author writes, "As you've probably figured out for yourself, I'm reluctant to say whether my evolving project is fiction or nonfiction, novel or memoir, science fiction or romance, hello or goodbye. A little tweaking and maybe it would fit in one category or the other. On the other hand, the hand supposed to keep track of what the other's doing, that tweaking, those categories one might say, are what I've been writing about, or trying to write my way out of, not only the last few years, but since the beginning" (136). This consciousness of genre coupled with a resistance to it is precisely what constitutes Wideman's career, and yet there is a sense in *Fanon* that his constant negotiation with the nature of literature and his place in it has exhausted him. *Fanon* is largely a book about the difficulty of writing.

Even more pointedly, it is about the difficulty of being John Edgar Wideman. There is a sense that his will to write is fading. He addresses Fanon in the opening pages, claiming that the activist was an inspiration and model early in Wideman's career: "it began clearly enough as a determination to be like you, that is, to become a writer committed to telling the truth about color and oppression. . . . Over the years I gradually resigned myself to the fact that I couldn't measure up to your example, and my Fanon project shifted to writing about disappointment with myself and my country, about shame and guilt and lost opportunities, about the price of not measuring up to announced ideals" (4). He is consumed not only with a sense of failure, but with the knowledge that he is aging and the suspicion that he is irrelevant: "I realize time's running out. I won't be writing many more books, if any. . . . Once upon a time I believed fiction writing was a privileged, not a suspect activity. . . . Writing fiction marginalized me" (5). *Hoop Roots* is about a subject that he had been thinking about his entire life, whereas *Fanon* is about a subject he had once felt a strong desire to write about but had deferred. Tellingly, he aspires not to tell the familiar story of Fanon but rather to focus on his last days in an American hospital, where Wideman's mother met the famous revolutionary (though the encounter may be invented and certainly allows Wideman's imagination to take over).

Imagination and reality participate in an intense, complex relationship throughout the book, beginning with the epigraph. To tell Fanon's story, which really does not begin until the book is more than halfway done, Wideman must deeply examine his own identity as a writer, including his career-long obsessive subjects. He also invents an alter-ego in a writer named Thomas. Thomas's plot begins with his receiving a package containing a severed head. This grotesque incident must be read metaphorically, though it can mean many things. (Severed heads recur throughout the novel, often as literary motifs, and have been featured in Wideman's other works, such as the story "Damballah"). Given the fact that Wideman examines himself so thoroughly in the novel, it is clear that the head is at least partially a symbol of his own alienation and a manifestation of the horrors of both his personal life and the broader history through which he has lived. Thomas (the alter-ego novelist) reads the gruesome symbol as a warning that he needs to confront the horror in his life, or in his own head. His musings about the meaning of the severed head (which may not in fact be a severed head, but rather a flight of fancy as he contemplates an unopened package) occupy his thoughts to the point that he cannot move forward, and thus it may be a metaphor for Wideman's own overactive, analytical mind that prevents him from writing a straightforward work of prose. The line between Wideman's own life and Thomas's fictional one blurs, yet the common denominator is that they both feel alienated from the facts of their past. Fanon, at least in the novel's early pages, is a distant figure indeed.

The book about Fanon exists first as an intermittent product of Thomas's rambling imagination, then as a film project the author pitches to the avant-garde French director Jean-Luc Godard. Interspersed with these motifs are lengthy philosophical musings and conversations with Wideman's brother Robby and with his mother, the two people who know about his plan to write a book about Fanon. As should be apparent, Wideman has no problem with violating the rules of fiction in this novel, and he acknowledges that anachronisms are rife, that the reader will not encounter a traditional narrative arc, and that to imagine the novel as a film script is completely permissible.

He figures Fanon as his jailer, presumably because Fanon will not let go of his imagination. This move causes him to meditate again on his brother's incarceration, and on its broader implications about the staggering number of black men in America's prisons. It is nearly an accident, he feels, that he is not the one in prison: "This scene I'm writing could be my brother visiting me, the two of us side by side just as we sit today, myself, my brother, one declared guilty, one declared innocent, variables in an invariant formula, but me in his place, him in mine, our fates switched, each of us nailed in our separate compartment of this hardass bench" (50–51). Part of this perspective can be attributed to fatalism, but part stems from the sense that he lacks control: "Almost thirty years ago I tried to write a book I hoped might free my brother from a life sentence in the penitentiary. It didn't work. Everything written after that book worked even less" (52). These morose feelings intensify when Robby tells him, essentially, to stop coming as the visits are damaging him psychologically. The status of this particular visit is painful, given that John and the reader know it is likely to be the last one with their ailing mother. The conversation is by turns mundane and morbid, and has little to do with Fanon until Robby asks, "How's your Fanon book coming. . . . You still writing about him, or is it the other one about the head" (63). John answers that it is about Fanon, but he does so without conviction. Robby praises his determination: "Bro, I got to hand it to you, man. You keep writing those buggy books. Always fussing cause you say nobody reads them, but you keep writing them. I dig it" (64).

Like his brother's perseverance in prison, Wideman's writing has devolved into pure survival. His identity becomes unstable as he imagines himself not as a writer but as someone who blends into his landscape almost passively. His obsession with Shakespeare's *The Tempest* had brought him to the figure of the dark-skinned prisoner Caliban in *The Island: Martinique.* In *Fanon* he relates more to Prospero, who is often interpreted as a stand-in for Shakespeare himself at the end of his career: "Prospero snapping his wand. Appalled by his career's tail end, the gathering darkness of any career winding down. All those pretty candles lit one by one with so much care and hopefulness, then one by one they gutter out, and when you peek over your shoulder, the room's just as black as when you started" (80). He reflects sourly on Fanon's diminished reputation: "Fanon's story remains relatively untouched, forgotten like novels on the bestseller list the year he died. Or the list from twenty years ago. Five years. Two years ago. Who could name one of those fabulously reviewed, avidly purchased books" (86). In the book's saddest moment, he responds to an audience member's question "Why do you write?" automatically, in a way he never has before: "I write because I'm lonely" (184). Alienation has been a feature of Wideman's writing from the outset. Here he leaves no question that his own feelings of alienation have all but subsumed him.

A book that contains a writer's struggle, his brother's despair in prison, his mother's impending death, a recurring severed head, and a forgotten revolutionary on his deathbed becomes coherent when alienation is recognized as its true subject. Art—Wideman's writing or Godard's films—seeks to examine the condition of alienation and even to intensify it rather than to posit a cure for it. The novel reaches a fever pitch, then reveals its own weariness. Robby continues to do his time. The fictional Thomas throws the severed head in a river. Fanon dies alone in a hospital. The author concludes his book with a letter to his mother in which he promises, "Will try to write soon again" (227). Given what he reveals about the difficulty of writing here, coupled with the fact of his diminished output since *Fanon,* one might conclude that his efforts were not altogether successful.

Fanon may or may not represent the "guttering out" of Wideman's career, but it (along with the other three "mash-ups" discussed in this chapter) is an important chapter in Wideman's development as an artist. Of the four, *Hoop Roots* was the only one that received much positive critical attention when it was published, but the more recent works have begun to attract substantial literary analysis. In them Wideman demonstrates his willingness to create his unique style, using various subjects to explore virtually everything that is on his mind.

Wideman's most recent book, *Writing to Save a Life: The Louis Till File,* brings together many of the themes discussed here and in some ways consolidates the major themes of his career. It even opens the way his first novel opens, with Wideman's recollection of a ride on his grandfather's shoulders through Homewood, just as Eddie Lawson did in *A Glance Away.* The character Clement, who swept the local barbershop and who is a major character in *Hiding Place,* is again featured here, framing the narrative at the beginning and end of the book. A significant moment in *Writing to Save a Life* is Wideman's loss of virginity on his grandmother's couch, an incident he explored earlier in the story "Backseat," and also central to this recent work is his trip south with his father as well as is the incarceration of his brother and son.

These familiar concerns may make it seem as though this book has little to do with its ostensible subject, the short, unhappy life of Louis Till, the father of Emmett Till, whose murder was a catalyst for the civil rights movement. Wideman's readers should be familiar with this technique, though: he has both tried to recover the story of Louis Till—as he has done with other African American men who are absent from history books—and attempted to explore deeply the intersections of his own life and Till's. As is the case with *Fanon,* one of his primary concerns here has been to demonstrate the necessary struggle of writing itself. The subtitle "Writing to Save a Life" can refer to many lives: Till's, Robby's, Jacob's, and his own. This concern is made explicit late in the book: "I work for an incarcerated son and brother. They are locked inside me, I am imprisoned with them during every moment that I struggle with the Till file. No choice. Trying to find words to help them. To help myself" (164).

The file is a set of documents Wideman obtained from the U.S. government through the Freedom of Information Act. Stationed in Europe during World War II, Till was convicted of raping an Italian woman and was executed. The purported facts of Till's case did not provide Wideman with the information he needed to tell his story, and the file itself was a mess when it arrived in Wideman's mailbox. It was not organized chronologically, and it omitted as much information as it contained. Its confidential status had been lifted when Emmett was murdered. Wideman has never asserted with conviction that Louis Till did not commit the crime that he was accused of committing, but the central section of the text points to inconsistencies that serve to destabilize the government's case, which he has described as "messy, all sort, gooey circumstantial evidence. Problematic at best" (162). The unexpressed corollary would be "Criminally erroneous at worst."

The text contains some lawyerly detective work on Wideman's part, but it is ultimately much more complex than just an inquiry into a sloppy case. Wideman's lifelong project has been to arrive at a sophisticated understanding of the relationship between fiction and the truth. He occasionally spins the reader's head around with statements such as this one: "Nothing closer to truth than truth—but the truth is—not even truth is close to truth. So we create fiction" (34). This urge to create allowed Wideman to visualize possible scenarios from Louis Till's life, including the night of the rape, but he has pondered the suspect ethics of doing so, wondering if he has been unscrupulous because he is "reporting imagination as fact" (152). In a book that interrogates the integrity of legal processes, his own act as a writer has left him "guilty" in two senses of the word: "I'm guilty of imagining pictures, sounds, words. Mine. I make them up. They could or could not be the way. It happened. Truth" (119). This halting, divided final sentence reinforces the doubt in his own writing that Wideman indicated in *Fanon,* like Prospero's candles guttering out.

Although he has expressed frustration with his own project throughout *Writing to Save a Life,* saying how it has stalled and indicating that it has left him with more questions than answers, and although it took him many years to complete what is one of his shorter books, Wideman persisted and ultimately managed to produce a book. Because of his deep need to understand his experiences and memories and because his mind is analytical by nature, the raw material for his writing is bottomless. There are slight revisions to the stories he has told before, as when his first lover, Latreesha, is named, and he has realized for the first time that this memorable tryst coincided with his traumatic memory of seeing the image of Emmett Till's destroyed face: "Latreesha's visit and Emmett Till's murder were the same treacherous summer, each boxed in a separate set of memories and associations until it dawns on me that they shared 1955" (70). His writing always offers the possibility of discovery: on trying to reconstruct the rocky relationship between Louis Till and his wife, Mamie, Wideman was compelled to reconstruct the night when his own father beat up his mother. Yet doubts exist as to whether his memory has been accurate when he has recalled the words his father uttered that night, wondering if they might have actually originated in a blues song or in banter he heard at a barbershop, "words dreamed, heard before the fact or after the fact of my mother's body striking the floor" (30). Secrets from his past had never been confessed until the publication of this late work, such as the fact that he once hid in the barbershop spying on Clement, terrified by this silent figure who has been re-created in many of his works.

Because the Till file was inadequate as source material for Wideman to reconstruct the man's life, he traveled to France to visit the grave where Till is buried. This reminded him of stories he heard of Emmett Till's grave being robbed, the famous glass-topped coffin now home to a family of possums. Louis Till's grave offered him little in terms of additional source material, but it caused him to come to terms with the eloquence of silence. The Till project led him to realize that words are not always adequate means of communication: "If I meet Louis Till eye to eye, and he chooses not to utter a single word, I would understand that I was being addressed by his silence. Understand that much more than words at stake" (140). The silent figure of Clement returns at the end of the book to remind Wideman that silence, absence, and gaps in stories are important: "Words are insufficient, much too late for only words. I must respect Till's absence. His silence. I must begin with doubled silences, absences. His. My own. Lost words, unspoken words. His. Mine" (191). For Wideman, as a writer, words are the substance of his identity. By the end of this work, he has arrived at an understanding of their limitation, but has also managed to express that idea in language, even though he does so in a way that indicates an understanding that his own eventual silence is inevitable.

CHAPTER 7

Wideman's Short Fiction

Despite the fact that his hybrid forms defy categorization, it is likely that Wideman will always be remembered primarily as a novelist and a memoirist, but he has been a consistent (even prolific) short story writer.[1] Since a frequent subject of Wideman's longer fiction and nonfiction is storytelling, it is not surprising that he is also adept at the short story form. Some of his novel chapters can stand alone as short stories, and his hybrid-form works *Hoop Roots* and *The Island: Martinique* each contain a short story as one chapter (both collected in *God's Gym*). In his introduction to *The Best American Short Stories of 1996,* building to his oft-repeated Igbo proverb "All stories are true," he says. "Stories that don't acknowledge the mystery at the center of things, don't challenge the version of reality most consenting adults rely upon day by day, are stories that disappear swiftly into the ever-present buzz of entertainment. Stories that do mount a challenge to our everyday conventions and assumptions stir my blood" (xx). Clearly this definition applies to his stories as well, as he has done all he can to avoid bland commercialism while mounting various challenges to everyday conventions. Laurie Champion has argued that "Wideman's stories keep people alive, while also challenging racism and employing both postmodern and cultural storytelling techniques."[2] Byerman, in a book-length study of Wideman's short fiction, argued that "he creates open-ended tales that express a desire for moral order but are skeptical about its achievement."[3]

In addition to *Damballah* (see chapter 3), Wideman has published four collections of stories. *Fever* appeared in 1989 at the end of his most productive decade. According to Byerman, these stories "blend tradition and experimentation, the past and the present, history and fiction" while "giving special attention to the problems of meaning and storytelling."[4] Five of the twelve stories had previously appeared in various magazines and journals. One story in *Fever,* "Presents," contains a self-conscious pronouncement that serves as a fitting introduction to his short fiction of this period: "The story has more skins than an onion. And like an onion it can cause a grown man to cry when he starts to peeling it" (101). Wideman's stories, like his longer fiction, are layered and tragic, and they reflect his characteristic traits: authenticity of voice, experimentation with structure, and attention to the act of storytelling itself. Working in a more concentrated form allows Wideman to focus on imagery and on the voices of characters to advance an idea economically. His longer works contain multiple, complex ideas, but the short fiction tends to select one idea and focus intently on it.

In *Fever* the stories can be grouped into three basic types: stories about stories, stories about history or memory, and stories about women. These categories are not absolute: some stories could fit into two or all three of them. Stories about stories sometimes focus on the rhythms of oral storytelling, as in "Little Brother," a conversational dialogue between two women named Penny and Geraldine that meanders between related but diverse topics such as dog ownership, love between spouses, and racial discrimination. This story rejects the traditional story arc with its clear conflict, rising action, and resolution in order to allow the voices of characters to dictate a story's shape.

Other stories about storytelling tend to be more experimental in the way they shift points of view, such as the opening story in the collection, "Doc's Story," about a legendary blind basketball player. On one level, it is less Doc's story than that of a nameless protagonist who hears the story. In the aftermath of a failed relationship with a woman, he goes to the basketball court for companionship, specifically to hear the "circle of stories" (2) that are passed around along with bottles of sweet wine and joints while players wait for their turn on the court: "the [story] about Doc had bothered him the most. Its orbit was unpredictable. . . . stories began with Doc and ended with Doc and everything in between was preparation, proof the circle was unbroken" (3, 4). In this way Doc's story is the urtext, not unlike the stories of Sybela Owens, John French, or Wideman's brother Robby in his other works. Doc had become famous for being able to sink free throws despite his blindness. For the denizens of the basketball court, he is a model of intuition and a kind of oracle. On the Sunday of the story, he misses a free throw and a young player turns the miss into a flashy slam dunk. Doc verbally puts the kid in his place and decides to actually play in the next game. For the story's protagonist, the tale of a wise aging blind man playing basketball is a story of the beliefs and values of his people. He wonders how his ex-lover, who is white, would react to the story: "Would the idea of a blind man playing basketball get her attention or would she have listened the way she listened when he told her stories he'd read about slavery days when Africans could fly, change themselves to cats and hummingbirds, when black hoodoo priests and conjure queens were feared by powerful whites even though ordinary black lives weren't worth a penny. To her it was folklore, superstition" (10). To him, it is clearly more. Their relationship seemed doomed to fail just as Doc seemed fated to end his basketball career when he lost his vision, but the story is about possibility and miraculous reversals. Despite the strength of his belief in Doc's story, the narrator wonders whether his relationship could have been saved if his lover had heard it. The story raises larger questions about racial cooperation in a world in which the stories of a minority are devalued by the majority.

Blindness is featured again in "When It's Time to Go," a story that begins with an animated teller and a willing listener sitting in a bar. The griot tells of a boy named Sambo who was born blind but also with a caul over his head, an omen that portends that the child will be a visionary. Unlike Doc, he is born without sight but begins to gain it. Just as suddenly as it arrives, his vision diminishes. A white doctor prescribes a medical treatment, but the community, who thinks his mother is a witch with magical powers, does not understand why she declines to heal him using alternative methods. Her way of expressing her love for her son is to send him away from home. The story abruptly changes to first person, with Sambo as the teller of the tale. He narrates his journey to New Orleans, where he played piano, and the story shifts to first person again, now with the auditor as the tale teller, who ends by stating the point of the story, wondering all along whether the story needs a point to be effective. The point is to get the reader to think about empathy: if we can imagine our blood in someone else's veins, and if we can imagine their hands playing music, the narrator prompts, we should shut our eyes tightly and ask ourselves "if something's been taken away or something given" (90). As with Doc in "Doc's Story," a character who is considered to be lacking something fundamental may actually possess gifts we can only imagine. These stories are variations on the way Wideman pays attention, recurrently, to characters whom others dismiss, notably his brother Robby.

The story "Surfiction" is an esoteric and postmodern take on storytelling. It reads more like an academic treatise than a story, playing with footnotes and marginal glosses on literary texts. The narrator begins with a set of interpretations about a Charles Chesnutt story, pondering the nature of authenticity in a voice at the center of the tale, but he pulls back and wonders if his own works are too imitative of postmodern masters such as Barthes, Borges, and

Barthelme. He imagines he is losing readers with every word, but he presses on. In classic postmodern form, the story interrupts its own flow constantly, calling attention to the expectations and demands of readers. The story struggles to clarify its aims as Wideman introduces himself as a character and invents (or utilizes) two characters, a married couple who are students in each of his two classes at the University of Wyoming and whose diaries form what would seem to be the core of the story, but he cannot sustain anything like a traditional narrative. Inevitably the plot breaks down and the characters vanish: "The stability of the narrative voice is displaced into a thousand distracted madmen screaming in the dim corridors of literary history" (69). He concludes with an allusion to Kurt Vonnegut's *Slaughterhouse Five*—"And so it goes" (69)—a phrase uttered repeatedly in Vonnegut's novel to indicate the absurdity of human existence. The story's playfulness belies Wideman's serious point about the self-conscious fiction he often produces: the more conscious we become about stories that mean something, the more difficult it is to write them. This may be a comment on his pre–Homewood Trilogy works that were aware of literary history to the point that it threatened to obscure the stories that mattered deeply to him.

The stories in the collection that are primarily about memory are considerably varied. "Rock River" is unusual in the Wideman canon in terms of voice, characterization, setting, and theme. It is the first-person narrative of a man who cleans up a truck in which a friend named Rick has shot himself. In his dialogue with Rick's widow Sarah, the suicide's life is gradually revealed. He was a hard drinker, who caused Sarah a good deal of grief. As the narrator looks into Sarah's eyes, he recalls a party and simultaneously sees an apparition of Rick walking in on the present scene, still drunk, asking why the narrator has the keys to his truck. Memory is a complex thing here as it prevents the narrator from clearly distinguishing the past from the present. He is haunted, but the portrait of the ghost is incomplete and imagistic. The reader, perhaps mirroring the feelings of the narrator, does not know whether to mourn the loss of Rick or to feel relieved by it. The story "Concert" continues some of the same motifs as the narrator blurs space and time. The story vacillates between a phone call and a jazz concert. The phone call contains bad news about the narrator's mother, and the story's evasiveness might be an attempt to stave off bad news, to suggest that something that has already happened can be deferred into a vague future. The narrator tells of how he has experienced a dream before of such a phone call and concert, which further destabilizes the reality of this tale and the reliability of its narrator.

Death also affects the story "Presents," whose title might be a pun on "presence." It is a complex series of memories about a protagonist and his grandmother. When he was seven, she gave him the present of a guitar on Christmas Eve, and his present to her was a promise to sing a Christmas song to her the next day. However, she dies during the night. Before dying, she had offered a deathbed prophecy that may parallel Wideman's own role as an artist: "she lays out the sad tale of his life as a man. He'll rise in the world, sing for kings and queens but his gift for music will also drag him down to the depths of hell" (99). Art that may please or enlighten its audience can also be a source of torment to the artist. In this case, the prophecy comes true: the remainder of the story, told mostly in the first person, is about how the narrator rises and falls repeatedly and how he tells his story hoping to break the pattern, hoping that there will be someone other than his grandmother to affirm his existence.

The longest story in the collection is the title story, "Fever," which trains its eye on history and memory. To a large degree, it reads like a rehearsal for the novel *The Cattle Killing,* but it emphasizes ideas more than character. It is a dense story, challenging for anyone not familiar with Wideman's work in general and *The Cattle Killing* in particular. But its essence can be gleaned by the casual reader: it is a story about the intersection of contagion and the treatment of black bodies historically. Wideman has drawn connections between the eighteenth-century Philadelphia plague and its contemporary equivalent—AIDS—both of which were attributed in the paranoid popular imagination to the importation of disease from Africa. Yet many other ideas adhere to the notion of fever as well: one of its narrators, Abraham, says, "Fever grows in the secret places of our hearts, planted there when one of us decided to sell one of us to another" (133). The contagion of racism, like the story, is not confined to a single time or place.

The stories about women in *Fever* cover the spectrum from women as strong, fully realized characters to women as sex objects with little agency over their fate or their depiction. "The Statue of Liberty" is an example of the latter. It begins at a distance from its human subjects, commenting indifferently on the houses that populate a certain landscape, but the narrator reveals himself to be a jogger who indulges in fantasies about what happens behind closed doors. He projects alternative identities and becomes a diminutive white woman running through a supposedly dangerous part of town. The story abruptly pivots to include two joggers—a white woman and a black man—who run together. The story is now narrated by a woman who watches them from one of the houses they jog past. It becomes a long and graphic seduction fantasy in which one white woman seduces a black man and his white wife. It is one of the most sexually explicit scenes Wideman has published, and the intent of the story is unclear, except that the liberty of the title connotes a freedom that is absent from the story's pages. It is a confining story with the fates of its characters completely controlled by the fantasy of the narrator. Its final image, not a comforting one, is of the ghost of a woman who rises nightly over a local pond to sing. Sex in this story is not liberating, and it is unclear whether storytelling or singing are either.

"Valaida" is one of Wideman's stories that has appeared in literature anthologies. Wideman's notes at the end of the volume indicate that the title character is based on a historical figure, Valaida Snow, "a jazz trumpeteer, singer, and dancer of immense talent" (163). The story begins with Valaida and a man named Bobby in heaven (a familiar Wideman motif), with Valaida giving an overview of her life. The most significant aspect of it is that she saved a boy in a concentration camp, though she did not know what happened to him afterwards. The remainder of the story is narrated by that boy, now grown into an adult in the United States named Mr. Cohen. He tells his version of the story to his black housekeeper, Clara Jackson. The story is profoundly meaningful to him—how Valaida sacrificed her own body to end his suffering as the Nazis were beating him—but Clara seems distant as he tells it, preoccupied with the details of her own life. He focuses on her indifference, on the way she is "lost in the cloud of her own noise" (39), and cannot complete his story; but he thinks it is more or less done anyway. His final vision unites them as he projects himself into Clara's world, able to overcome differences between race, gender, and religion in order to consider her part of his family. It is the act of telling Valaida's story that enables him to get over his survivor's guilt and to recognize the broad importance of the woman's sacrifice. From Valaida's perspective in heaven, however, her message was contained in her music, in her trumpet solos and in one lyric: "Dear Lord above, send back my love" (29). Hope for humanity comes in sometimes indescribable reactions to sacrifice and generosity.

"Hostages" is a much more complex story that also deals with a Jewish protagonist, one whose lifelong history of relationships with people darker than herself cause her to wonder, in the story's conclusion, "how many dark lives must be sacrificed" (57). The story's challenges come from its shifting point of view, its tendency to move quickly across time via memory, and the complexity of its nameless protagonist. She found her relationship with her first husband vexing because he was an Arab. Her role as a mother causes some anxiety in her, and her dreams are haunted by corpses and threats. The story is a gathering of snapshots from her life, arranged unpredictably, revealing emotions and motifs rather than a coherent point. A hostage is someone who creates an unwilling sacrifice, for whom the terms of sacrifice are determined by another. She builds on this observation to try to figure out her feelings of dependence and isolation, her struggles to connect to others who do not share her history. As in "Valaida," there is common ground between the historical suffering of black people and

Jews, but the fragmented nature of this story makes it more difficult to discern whether any healing follows this understanding.

One story, "The Tambourine Lady," is about a young girl rather than a woman, specifically about her crisis of faith occasioned by the confluence of her anticipation of going to church and her memories of walking home from school. The walk home from school is fraught with anxiety because a boy she loves name Tommy Bonds has shoved her down to the sidewalk. This event is especially terrifying in that she was avoiding the cracks in the sidewalk because of the childhood superstition that stepping on them will break her mother's back. She is also consumed by the story of a young girl who was hit by a car and by the fact she once told Tommy her secret (though the reader never learns it). The story's imagery largely connotes falling and breaking, and there is a parallel between these actions and the tension between salvation (church) and damnation (the streets). Like many of Wideman protagonists, she senses a doubleness in her life and dimly understands that the portal between her separate worlds is language: "Words like doors. You open one wide and peek inside and everybody in there, strolling up and down the red aisles, singing, shaking hands. . . . Words like the [jumping] rope right on time slapping the pavement, snapping her heart" (111, 112). The story has no clear resolution, but like many others in this collection, it reveals an acute awareness of the way language has the power to connect.

Guzzio argued that *Fever* is a good example of why reading one of Wideman's works in isolation is less productive than reading his entire oeuvre: "On its own, the collection is still a display of Wideman's virtuoso narrative styles, but without the context of Wideman's other work, it is more difficult to comprehend how it fits into Wideman's artistic vision" (39). As many of Wideman's critics are aware, his complex vision cannot be gleaned by reading a single work. And yet there is a danger that his stories in particular might be overlooked by less committed readers, especially given the fact that Wideman apparently uses some as rehearsals for longer works or actually replaces them within other works (as he did with the story "Tommy" in *Sent for You Yesterday,* which is altered only slightly as it becomes part of the novel *Hiding Place*). This tendency is best viewed as revision as opposed to recycling.

Even book titles are subject to revision: Wideman's 1992 collection *All Stories Are True* was originally published under the title *The Stories of John Edgar Wideman*. It is a return to the family stories he explored in the Homewood books and in his memoirs. The first three stories in this collection as well as the final one are directly based on Wideman's personal experience, and the subjects are familiar ones: incarceration, the decline of Homewood, memory, and the perseverance of his strong relatives. The title is an African saying that

Wideman has suggested can mean many things, but one connotation is that these "true stories" are fictionalized but close to reality. The remaining stories in the collection are diverse in terms of their themes, subjects, and methods of storytelling. In stark contrast with the nearly nonfictional tone of the personal stories, "Loon Man" is a dark myth, almost a horror story. "Everybody Knew Bubba Riff" is an experiment in stream of consciousness: it is one long sentence that carries the reader along on its swift current. If the stories have anything in common despite their diversity, it is that they are dark, even for Wideman. The collection was published in 1992, six years after his son was arrested and eight years before the end of his thirty-five-year marriage. It was clearly a turbulent time for him personally, and the darkness of his circumstances is reflected in these pieces.

The first two stories in the collection emphasize an evolving truth about Wideman: he is more comfortable discussing his brother Robby's crime and incarceration than he is discussing his son Jacob's circumstances. The opening story, "All Stories are True," begins with the protagonist in conversation with his mother, who is too weary that day to visit her son Tommy in prison. As the narrator revisits Homewood, he chants the names of the streets like an incantation, "sorrow and loss in every syllable when you say them to yourself" (6). The story builds on this feeling of decay and nostalgia: his mother is weary not only because she has been visiting Tommy in prison for many years with no change in his condition but also because she is elderly and has undergone treatment for cancer. Yet there seems to be hope for renewed life as well: her hair, for instance, has begun to grow back after the chemo treatments. A similar seesawing of emotions is evident when the narrator visits Tommy in jail. Like other renditions of Robby in Wideman's work, Tommy in this story is resilient and has managed to thrive despite his desperate surroundings. He tells a poignant story of a leaf carried on a current of wind near the prison wall. The prisoners gather to cheer on the leaf, and they collectively celebrate when it blows over the wall, a symbol of the freedom they desire. But the story's abrupt conclusion reverses the meaning of the tale; Tommy says, "I'm gonna tell you something I don't tell nobody when I tell about the leaf. The dumb thing blew back again" (16). For the reader of Wideman's oeuvre, the power of Robby/Tommy is his ongoing optimism, and although that optimism is evident in this story, Wideman's own willingness to believe in the future may be wearing down.

The next story in the collection, "Casa Grande," takes on the mostly taboo subject of his son's incarceration, but it moves away from his son as a character quickly. The story begins by reprinting a story the narrator's son wrote when he was ten years old. He is now twenty-one and serving a life sentence in Arizona. The narrator admits, "I was attempting to write in my journal about the way it feels when the terrible reality of his situation comes down on me, when I exchange for a fraction of a second my life for his. Longer than that I can't bear" (19). The story—the shortest in the collection—is evidence that Wideman cannot sustain an engagement with Jacob's crime and incarceration in his writing any more than he can in life. It retreats into a year-old journal entry that emerges from the imagination much more than from reality, and it ends even more abruptly than "All Stories are True," though with a similar image: of angels (rather than a leaf) plummeting to earth. The final story in the collection, "Welcome," is more evidence of Wideman's difficulty in writing about Jacob. It again takes up the figure of Wideman's grieving mother in the throes of chemotherapy, and though it is largely narrated from the point of view of one of Wideman's sisters, the author's voice returns in the final paragraph. He proclaims to his sister, "I'm no crier," but he becomes emotional when he witnesses a pathetic scene of a too-young father and his tearful son at a bus stop. He admits how much he misses his son, "and then I had to cry some more" (142).

"Backseat," the longest story in the collection, contains little that would encourage the reader to label it fiction. The reader of Wideman's work encounters familiar names and family anecdotes, and the author is referred to as "Doot" as he was in the last book of the Homewood Trilogy. Wideman has described it as a "dirge" that he wrote when his grandmother was ailing, a story filled with "loss and absence and regret."[5] The story begins, though, not with his relatives but with his memory of repeatedly copulating in the back seat of his uncle's car as a teenager with a girl named Thomasina. The sex is not described romantically, but it turns into a story that he shares with Thomasina and a friend named Scott now that they are adults. In retrospect, these sexual episodes with neither the outcome nor the desire for procreation serve the purpose of unburdening Wideman and enabling him to return to the foundational stories of his ancestry. The story spools out into a series of memoir-like meditations on his ancestors, their names, and the way their legacy has contributed to his personality. He feels guilt that he did not visit his grandmother before her death and is led to the memory of the first time he made love, not coincidentally in his grandmother's house. He is thrilled and terrified by his first sexual experience and imagines that the stain he and his lover have left on his grandmother's couch will transform into a baby, but it fades to nothing. He is relieved, but the image suggests the impermanence of individual lives. Yet this memory leads back to the initial memory of sexual pleasure in the backseat of his uncle's car, and the cyclical nature of stories and memory partially balances the linear nature of life.

One of the more poignant stories in the collection in terms of the troubled racial world that Wideman chronicles is "Signs," about a black, female professor at a southern university who is being threatened and harassed. The protagonist, Kendra Crawley, initially returns home to her doting aunts who fuss over her and frame her in such a way that she feels she is the center of the universe, but she harbors plenty of self-doubt even as she accepts their attention. This scene is redolent with imagery of a fallen, post-Edenic world, and Kendra is well aware of its debased condition even as she accepts her aunts' belief that she is perfect. The idea of a fallen Eden carries over into her world as a professor since she is teaching *Paradise Lost,* and one of her white students claims not to understand it. In her mind she reveals her insecurities, which stem from the fact that this student is challenging her and that she is compelled to teach the great white works of Western civilization rather than classics from the black tradition. The student's status as a white male undermines the hierarchy she has achieved through her professional status, making the authority a professor holds in relation to a student seem flimsy. She fantasizes about what she would like to tell the student, but she ends up smiling and politely sticking to her role as the patient instructor. She recalls her own time in college when her white, male professor responded to her essay with a giant red X on the first page and a huge question mark on the last. She thinks, "Those marks he put on my paper, Mama, it was as if he'd tattooed my body. Scarlet slashes on my chest. Rusty iron hook in my back. Felt like I was walking around naked and everybody could see. Everybody knew. This nigger gal don't belong here" (79). This trauma carries forward into her adult life, and the line between fantasy and reality is blurred as she copes with her student. Signs begin appearing on campus: the first, which says, "Whites Only," is tacked to a bathroom even though she lives in "the post-emancipation, post-riots, post–civil rights, post–equal opportunity, post-modern last decade of the twentieth century" (80). The second sign is actually a note slipped under her door that reads, *"Nig bitch go home"* (83). The third is the letters KKK written in chalk on her door. After a dozen or more incidents, she contacts the dean of her school, who insists that they will investigate, though he pleads with her to help prevent the news of these threats from reaching the outside community.

The threats not only continue but intensify, and they become more sexually threatening as well as racially offensive. She had conjured a fantasy lover early in the story who "had the power to change the way she looked at herself" (80). She now imagines that the man harassing her is that lover but that he is evil and twisted, and she regards herself through his demented eyes. Kendra's mindset demonstrates the persistence of the concept of double-consciousness that DuBois advanced in 1903. The prejudices of the white world have affected her psychology on a deep level. She longs for her childhood, especially the times in church that made her feel innocent and protected, but the story suggests that a belief in such ideas is self-deceptive: her world has always been fallen, even if she once believed otherwise. Her internal struggle is laid bare. She does not know which voice in her head is deceiving her: the one calling her home or the one that lured her into this hostile world. It is not surprising when she confesses that she was the perpetrator of the threats against her. There is enough ambiguity at the story's conclusion to suggest she only confessed so she could move on, but her story acts as a parable of the condition of being black in the twentieth century. The theories of DuBois (who is named in the story) persist even after the advances of the struggles for civil rights in the 1950s and 1960s.

Two of the stories in the collection take the ethics of modern journalism as their subject. The first, "What He Saw," is Wideman's only work that takes place in Africa. It depicts the author (not named in this story) as one of a group of visitors to South Africa during the apartheid regime. He joins a videographer, two photographers, and a print journalist as they tour war-torn Soweto. Wideman has drawn an analogy between his writing and photography elsewhere, notably in *Reuben*. In this story his occasional unease with the role of a writer who dissects individual lives and holds them up for inspection has a parallel in the work of the photographers on the trip who "shoot" their subjects rather than take photographs of them. The violence of the apartheid regime is implicitly compared to the artistic violence that seeks to capture people's lives rather than help them or even genuinely interact with them. (Wideman's occasional anxiety over chronicling the experiences of his beleaguered brother and son is evident.) The story opens with the narrator's description of a photo he is holding from this trip. He admits he does not know the name of its subject and in fact does not know anything about him except that he has been shot. His emotional distance is mirrored in the very setup of the photo: "The light is flat and merciless. Distorted by the angle at which the camera was held" (96). He realizes how difficult it is to regard people as artistic subjects when you realize their pain and suffering.

The narrator's status as a foreigner enables him to attempt to describe the scene of a tragic South African slum with dispassion, but he understands the parallels between this world and his home in Pittsburgh as well as the American South, the site of the history that connects Pittsburgh and Africa. As in the blighted city of his youth, he senses a battle between the shabby materials that attempt to mark "the sacred space of family" and "gangs [that] prey on the weak" (99). It is a once-beautiful landscape that is now marked by waste and destruction. He wonders repeatedly what he and the journalists are doing here and questions with them the ethics of the first photo they shot, which depicts a young boy defecating by the side of the road. The narrator worries that they have violated the little privacy the boy had, but by retelling the anecdote in this piece he is doing the same thing. The photographer who took the boy's picture argues, "We got to tell their story" (102), presumably because poor South Africans do not have the means to tell their own. As a gun battle breaks out, the narrator's eyes begin to play tricks on him, and he is unsure whether he is clearly seeing the Africans in the landscape around them, giving poignancy to the title of the story: "What He Saw" makes the reader curious about what he did *not* see. The ethics of the boy's situation becomes murkier as the subject of the original photograph—a man shot during a rally—arrives and the journalists and narrator both fear for their lives at the hands of a hostile police force. Although they are intrusive and not immediately beneficial to the suffering citizens of South Africa, these individuals do have the power not only to see but to make others see as well. The story ends with the narrator watching them continue to take photographs, wondering what it is they see and whether they will help him see differently.

The story "Newborn Thrown in Trash and Dies" is also at the crossroads between art and journalism. Wideman encounters this particular true story as a news headline and uses it as an opportunity to examine a discarded life (again, recalling those of his brother and son) by animating the unfortunate infant who is in fact just one of a number of discarded babies discovered each year. The story takes the form of falling past ten stories of a building, the number that the infant in the news story was dropped. The floors start off as numbers but change to concepts such as the floor of facts, the floor of questions, and the floor of wishes. Wideman derives a great deal of artistic and philosophical license from this structure, and this story, like "What He Saw," frames an ethical dilemma: not the obvious one about the rejection of an infant by those who brought her into the world but a broader one about fate and the responsibility we all share for the lives of others. It cycles between an almost romantic sentimentality about the life not lived and its opposite: the possibilities that this life will include brutal victimization and sorrow, the latter when her brother (with the familiar name Tommy) is killed by gang violence. Like the earlier autobiographical stories in the collection, this one ends with a final plummet earthward: "Tommy is beginning to remember me. To join me where I am falling unseen through your veins and arteries down down to where the heart stops, the square opening through which trash passes to the compactor" (128). This bleak conclusion is merely an elaboration of the cold headline that is the title of the story, but Wideman uses it, as he often does, to make the reader consider the layers beneath the surface, even (or especially) if they make one uncomfortable.

As in his other late-career work, Wideman's stories of the 2000s tend to rely on free association to explore the intersection of lives. Like *All Stories Are True,* Wideman's 2005 collection *God's Gym* opens with an autobiographical story about his mother. It is honest about the blurry line between fact and fiction: Wideman reads the story in progress to his mother and says as an aside, "I called it a story but Mom knew better" (4). "Weight" is among the most revealing of Wideman's stories not only in terms of what he confesses—a love for his mother so intense that it renders him "a little crazy . . . tongue-tied, scared shitless" (15, 16) at the prospect of her death—but also in terms of his art. He regards his mother as his best critic, and he is pulled up short partway through this story when she responds with cold silence. He has joked about her ability to bear an uncanny amount of emotional weight, which leads to the phrase "God's Gym," which forms the title of the collection. He pictures that phrase on a T-shirt she might wear, signifying how her faith in God has enabled her to take on the burdens her children have heaped on her, John included (though in a different way from his siblings). Her silence and subsequent criticism lead him to doubt the merit of the beginning of the story and the efficacy of the metaphor he has created, but he also fears he has unconsciously attacked his mother, hurled a "stone I'd bull's-eyed right into the middle of her wrinkled brow" (6). He is guilty, and yet, he admits, "I couldn't deny a sneaky, smarting tingle of satisfaction at the thought that maybe, maybe words I'd written had touched another human being, mama mia or not" (7). He is still concerned with the ethics of being a writer; in this case, his guilt over interpreting his mother's experience is balanced by the writer's desire, even need, to continue to write even if it strains personal relationships. The metaphor of weight is one that he explains to her, but it operates in a number of ways, especially when he plays out his fear and imagines himself bearing the literal weight of his mother as he hefts her coffin at her funeral. He concludes that what upset her is not the metaphor of her as a weightlifter but rather his admission that he was "practicing for [her] death in a story" (13). This conclusion is complex, but it is the heart of the story and of Wideman's practice of speculating about what is unsaid and unseen. His mother's silence opens up his imagination, but it also encourages him to confess the idea that he has been keeping silent his whole life, that he has been "scared every cotton-picking day of my life I'd lose you" (15). He is nearly paralyzed, artistically, by the simultaneous need to describe the perfect synergy of his mother's life and his own, coupled with the fear of not getting it right.

Death and silence are the motifs that run throughout *God's Gym*. The narrator contemplates his own death in "Are Dreams Faster than the Speed of Light" after his doctors diagnose him with a terminal disease. The story is largely about his own father's impending death, though, providing a counterpart to "Weight." It is impossible not to associate the narrator with the author: he is a novelist named John Edgar, he is from Homewood, and his father—rendered silent in his old age because of a stroke—is named Edgar. The only plot of this memoir-like story is the narrator's conviction that his last duty on earth before dying is to speed up his father's inevitable death. He imagines poisoning him with hemlock, an allusion that connects to a painting he remembers about ancient Greek thinkers holding conversations with living philosophers. This mercy killing remains in the narrator's imagination, one of the dreams named in the title that can allow his mind to shuttle between the real and the fantastic. His final gesture is not to euthanize his father, however, but to nurture him: he spoon-feeds his father with determined concentration, because in spite of his broad-ranging meditations on the fleeting nature of existence, "nothing, nothing else matters" (70).

Wideman draws the grim conclusion that we are all living with the unspoken knowledge of death. This idea returns in "Who Weeps When One of Us Goes Down Blues": "Sooner or later, in one way or another, everybody goes down" (139). The "one of us" in the title could be taken to mean all people, but in the context of the story it refers first to a group of basketball players in an amateur league and then to African Americans. The narrator's mind embarks on a number of flights of fancy: "In this unfolding space nothing stays what it appears to be" (147). This transference describes the style of many of Wideman's late stories: one idea morphs into another seamlessly. The story ends up in ancient Africa, moves across time and space so that it has little to do with its original catalyst (the collapse of a player on a basketball court). As in the story of his father's impending death, though, the conclusion here is that the game goes on even after one player goes down. Death is the oversized subject of many of these stories, but it is possible to read them as Wideman's attempt to convince himself and the reader that individual deaths are insignificant.

The story "Hunters" intensifies Wideman's anxious explorations of race-mixing, carrying over the inquiry he began in "Signs" in his earlier collection. This story begins with a brutal scene in which white rednecks murder and rape a light-skinned black woman named Jill. The scene is disturbing and almost cartoonish in its depiction of the assailants, and Wideman moves from it into a rambling meditation on the nature of black hair, passing, and (finally) the anxiety black students face when they attend predominately white universities. He has to repeatedly refocus the story: it is Jill's, he insists, not his. Her goal was to assimilate, to make race disappear. The story examines fate, particularly the willingness to work against the fate ascribed to black individuals by a society prone to stereotyping. It is ultimately another story about the deep psychological effects of double-consciousness, and the rape that acts as the story's frame is meant to be a metaphor and also a product of his distorted imagination. He returns to the rape scene and reveals that it is just his own paranoid fantasy, that the blood is "only ketchup. It's only my green jealousy and red anger" (26). He apologizes to his ancestors "for telling tales in Babylon's tongue, stories full of Babylon's lies" (26), and vows to attend instead to Malcolm X's speeches, John Coltrane's saxophone solos, and other expressions of black hope.

In "The Silence of Thelonius Monk" he does attend deeply to the work of the legendary jazz pianist in order to get at the notion of silence, both within Monk's music and at the end of Monk's career. The story merges Wideman's own experience with the story of the star-crossed French poets and lovers Verlaine and Rimbaud and with Monk's legend. According to that legend, Monk refused to play piano by the end of his career, spending his time at local delis mumbling cryptic witticisms to the men he knew there. Verlaine and Rimbaud were involved in a public duel; in Wideman's version, Rimbaud recovers from his wound and sinks into silence as he migrates to the United States in the present day. Silence is a metaphor for death, but it is also one of Monk's languages, something the listener is supposed to attend to and figure out. Wideman admits, "I haven't delved into [my silence] very deeply yet, have I, avoid my silence like a plague, even though the disease I'm hiding from already rampant in my blood, bones, the air" (48). As he addresses his former lover, silence represents the possibilities of their past. Silence covers an unspoken plea for connection. As he tries to express this idea, the stories of Verlaine and Rimbaud and of Thelonius Monk continuously interrupt. Monk chides the author at the end for speaking for him: "Who said I retreated to silence? Retreat hell. I was attacking in another direction" (52). These words can be interpreted as a validation of Wideman's own growing tendency toward silence late in his career or as a way for him to emerge from silence and produce the words that create something out of the nothingness of the imagination.

Silence appears in the title of another story in the collection, "What We Cannot Speak About We Must Pass Over in Silence." It begins, "I have a friend with a son in prison" (93), indicating the subject that Wideman is least fond of addressing in his writing—his son Jacob's incarceration—and attributing it to a friend rather than to himself. The narrator reports that the friend has died, and he is left to meditate on why he is more empathetic to the imprisoned son than to the deceased friend, who was really just a casual acquaintance. The narrator becomes obsessed with locating the imprisoned son, a circumstance that gives Wideman the opportunity to insert a criticism of the cold, profit-driven logic of the prison-industrial complex. Once he locates the son, the narrator labors over the best way to express his condolences, but he receives the following curt reply: "Some man must have fucked my mother. All I knew about him until your note said he's dead. Thanks" (100). The story might have ended there, but since Wideman's stories are largely about the intersection of lives, the narrator continues, telling his own story about an affair he had with the paralegal who helped him find the friend's son in the Arizona prison. His story is also about his decision to claim that he is the father of the incarcerated young man when he visits him in prison. This decision would allow him to cut through the red tape associated with visiting prisoners, but it gets him thinking about the nature of parenthood. Given the subject of the story and the fact that Wideman chooses to kill off the character who claims to be the father, this subject is telling. Judging by this story, Wideman's feelings of devastation over Jacob's fate involve a complex combination of horror at the boy's crime and the father's unspeakable guilt. Defending the incarcerated son to his lover, the narrator says, "Everyone has crimes to answer for. . . . Suppose I said my crimes are more terrible than his" (114). As he enters the prison, he experiences a feeling of existential alienation as strong as the one his friend described at the beginning of the story, and he has an anxious vision that involves falling to his knees, "forced to recite my sins, the son's sins, the sins of the world" (118). His empathy with the son is not a declaration of the boy's innocence so much as a recognition that everyone is guilty, depraved, a criminal on some level.

The concluding story in the collection, "Sightings," again begins with silence and death. The narrator thinks he sees a colleague who had committed suicide years earlier, and this brief moment of mistaken identity sends his mind on a dizzying stream of consciousness sentence that lasts for pages. This beginning of one of Wideman's last substantial stories is a good introduction to the sheer force of his far-reaching mind. The story is about the workings of memory, how the past can seem more real than the present and yet in one's memory "each promising detail bodiless, the network of memories it spins out cannot hold, evaporates, brings back everything, nothing" (160). The breathless introductory sentence reads like a desperate attempt to give form and weight to ephemeral memories. As he meditates on the suicides of two old acquaintances, he becomes overwhelmed by the moments he experiences on a daily basis where past and present collide: "At these moments my life feels crowded and empty. I'm stalled at a crossroads with lots of traffic in many directions whirring around me and I can't regain my bearings, don't know how to step back into the flow" (163). His disorientation continues and deepens, and he realizes that his subject has become "coincidence," a word that carries many connotations for him but is mainly "a spinning universe intersecting with another spinning universe" (172). This definition describes much of his later work, and it invariably ends with a reversal of the beginning of the story: as a counterpart to seeing an old friend long dead, he becomes an invisible object whom an old friend looks right through as though he is not there.

One of the least Widemanesque stories in the collection is "Sharing," a dialogue-heavy tale about an encounter between two neighbors—a black man and a white woman—who have been living as strangers for years out of miscommunication and misinterpretation of one another. When the man asks to borrow mayonnaise from the woman, they finally engage in a conversation that allows them to realize how much they have in common. It is atypical of Wideman in its straightforward quality, its halting, almost stagey dialogue, and its nearly overt statement of its theme at the end. In short, it does not seem complex enough to be a Wideman story, and it can perhaps be read as a plea or desire for clarity in a private world that had grown knotty and disturbing by this point in the author's career.

Just when it seems like one can trace a pattern in Wideman's work, he abruptly changes. The oddness of "Sharing" paves the way for even odder takes on the short story in his most recent collection, *Briefs: Stories for the Palm of the Mind* (2010). *Briefs* is odd for two reasons: (1) because it is essentially self-published with Lulu books (where his son Daniel is an editor), and (2) because it contains one hundred pieces in the space of 155 pages. In an interview article in the *Los Angeles Times,* he said, "In the pace and rhythm of life we have around us today . . . it's a struggle to get a private minute. For me, the private minute is what it's all about. It's what a powerful culture like ours tends to crush."[6] This sentiment is hard to accept in a writer whose aesthetic demanded so much of his readers over the years: no other Wideman work could be digested in a series of private minutes. It seems more consistent with his tendency, late in his career, toward withdrawal. The silence he engages with as a theme in *God's Gym* surrounds these microfictions. They touch on familiar motifs, but they only explore those motifs in flashes.

A strong whiff of both self-consciousness and self-doubt runs through *Briefs.* In one piece Wideman announces his intention overtly: "Teaching myself to cut back on the ambition of long forms. Settling for the satisfaction of well-wrought miniatures" (70). While some of the pieces are indeed well-wrought miniatures, others are decidedly not: they read like notebook exercises more than carefully constructed and revised prose. He confesses at one point, "Sometimes I'm sad I'm not the best writer in the world" (31), but at other points he indicates that he is done trying to be, that the fight and competitive spirit that informed his playing basketball and his drive to succeed in the hostile world of Ivy League universities, as well as in his writing, have diminished along with the length of his works. The well-wrought miniatures in the collection are sprinkled amid stories that feel incomplete or like rough drafts. Homewood is not the setting of many of the briefs, and while some of his recurrent subjects (such as incarceration, basketball, death, and sex) are showcased here, there are also new subjects that are not as common in his earlier writing, notably political commentary (he describes himself as "an old man ashamed of this country" [15]) and his relationship with his second wife. It is fair to say that his increasing trend toward cynicism is fully on display here. One story about twins becomes a myth about how a feud escalates until "the sons and their sons and their son's sons, even unto the present generation, have waged murderous wars upon one another, perpetuating the slaughter and chaos that give humanity such a bad name" (20).

Perhaps because brevity gives Wideman an escape hatch, these tiny stories allow him to talk about Jacob as overtly as he does anywhere in his oeuvre. In "Writing (2)" he is left only with sadness and a feeling of helplessness, "the sadness that's most real when in fact it's not yours and can only be imagined, the way once upon a time in your dreams you imagined your children's lives might be perfect or at least a whole god damn lot better off than you'll ever be or do until one day you find yourself writing about an altogether different state of affairs than you ever would have imagined. And not very well" (31). The following story, "Thirteen," treats Jacob's crime and its effect on Wideman even more overtly. His sorrow and mystification are evident here; he even admits that he had "stopped loving" (32) Jacob's mother as they drove to Arizona to enter his guilty plea. The conclusion is gut-wrenching: "You only get one chance. That's all a father gets with a son. A child's life in your hands once. That's it. Once. He was born in New Jersey and I took classes to assist at his birth, but some clown passed out the day before, so on the 13th the delivery room off limits for fathers and I missed the moment the earth cracked and she squeezed out his bloody head" (33). Wideman's sense of failure and fatalism are strong here. The number thirteen—the date of Jacob's birth—is associated with bad luck, and his sentiment is not that he failed as a father but that he missed his "chance" because of circumstances beyond his control. This attitude seems less a way to explain what happened than a way to live with it. But the final story in the collection, "Shadow," is a single sentence: "He notices a shadow dragged rippling behind him over the grass, one more silent, black presence for which he's responsible" (155). One cannot help but interpret his willingness in "Thirteen" to blame his son's circumstances on matters out of his hands as a way to mask the imagery of this final "brief." While it may be a mere shadow, the fact that he is always dragging it proves how heavy it weighs on him.

The dominant note of many of the stories in *Briefs* involves emotional survival instead of anything as lofty as happiness. He frequently examines the ethics of being a writer, as in the story "Ruins," in which he includes his second wife's complaint that he writes about their personal lives too publicly. Rather than refrain from publishing descriptions of their private moments, he bonds with his reader, claiming that this instance "is a replay of numerous upsets with me when she confuses my fiction with our lives. What do you think, Dear Reader. Does she have a case" (49). The fact that he omits question marks from these last two questions suggests that he knows the answer. And yet, if one thing is consistent throughout Wideman's long, varied career, it is that he will write about what he wants to write about, in whatever form he wishes, despite any reader's resistance, even those readers who are close to him.

NOTES

Chapter 1: Understanding John Edgar Wideman

1. Wideman, preface, *The Homewood Trilogy,* vii.
2. TuSmith and Byerman, *Critical Essays on John Edgar Wideman,* xi.
3. Wideman, *Brothers and Keepers,* 29.
4. TuSmith, *Conversations with John Edgar Wideman,* 214.
5. Guzzio, *All Stories are True,* 4.
6. Abu-Jamal, "The Fictive Realism of John Edgar Wideman," 76.
7. Coleman, *Blackness and Modernism,* 4.
8. See Byerman, *John Edgar Wideman: A Study of the Short Fiction* and *The Life of Work of John Edgar Wideman;* Guzzio, *All Stories are True;* and TuSmith and Byerman, *Critical Essays on John Edgar Wideman.*
9. TuSmith, *Conversations with John Edgar Wideman,* 150.
10. Reed, *Airing Dirty Laundry,* 144.
11. Wideman, introduction, *Best American Short Stories of 1996,* xviii.
12. TuSmith, *Conversations with John Edgar Wideman,* 161, 172.
13. Byerman, *John Edgar Wideman: A Study of the Short Fiction,* xi.
14. Pearsall, "Narratives of Self and the Abdication of Authority in Wideman's *Philadelphia Fire,* 15.
15. TuSmith and Byerman, *Critical Essays on John Edgar Wideman,* viii.
16. TuSmith, *Conversations with John Edgar Wideman,* 23.
17. Byerman, *The Life and Work of John Edgar Wideman,* ix.
18. TuSmith, *Conversations with John Edgar Wideman,* 177.
19. Ibid., 22.
20. Chametsky, *Black Writers Redefine the Struggle,* 63.
21. TuSmith, *Conversations with John Edgar Wideman,* 135.
22. Wideman, "Doing Time, Marking Race," 504.
23. TuSmith, *Conversations with John Edgar Wideman,* 31.
24. Byerman, *John Edgar Wideman: A Study of the Short Fiction,* 26.
25. TuSmith, *Conversations with John Edgar Wideman,* 49.
26. Guzzio, *All Stories are True,* 42.

Chapter 2: The First Three Novels

1. TuSmith, *Conversations with John Edgar Wideman,* 50.
2. Ibid., 51.
3. Guzzio, *All Stories are True,* 5–11, 15–47.
4. TuSmith, *Conversations with John Edgar Wideman,* 44.

5. Roskolenko, "Junkie's Home," 56.
6. TuSmith and Byerman, *Critical Essays on John Edgar Wideman,* 93.
7. Guzzio, *All Stories are True,* 17.
8. TuSmith, *Conversations with John Edgar Wideman,* 5.
9. Ibid., 96.
10. Ibid., 7.
11. Guzzio, *All Stories are True,* 65.
12. TuSmith, *Conversations with John Edgar Wideman,* 11.
13. Leonard, "There is No Africa," 27.
14. Coleman, *Blackness and Modernism,* 25.
15. Guzzio, *All Stories are True,* 64.
16. Broyard, "A Lynching in Black Face," 37.
17. Coleman, *Blackness and Modernism,* 44.
18. Harris, *Exorcising Blackness,* 129, 141.
19. TuSmith and Byerman, *Critical Essays on John Edgar Wideman,* 110.
20. Ibid., 110.

Chapter 3: Homewood Bound

1. Coleman, *Blackness and Modernism,* 7.
2. See Denise Rodriguez, "Homewood's Music of Invisibility," in TuSmith and Byerman, *Critical Essays on John Edgar Wideman,* 127–40.
3. Coleman, *Blackness and Modernism,* 4.
4. Guzzio, *All Stories Are True,* 98.
5. TuSmith, *Conversations with John Edgar Wideman,* 16.
6. Ibid., 31.
7. Ibid., 18.
8. Ibid,. 26.
9. TuSmith, *Conversations with John Edgar Wideman,* 21.
10. Cheuse, "Homecoming in Homewood," 12.
11. TuSmith, *Conversations with John Edgar Wideman,* 18.
12. Guzzio, *All Stories Are True,* 132.

Chapter 4: Brothers and Fathers

1. Guzzio, *All Stories Are True,* 99.
2. Reed, "Of One Blood, Two Men," 33.
3. Byerman and TuSmith, *Critical Essays on John Edgar Wideman,* 3.
4. TuSmith, *Conversations with John Edgar Wideman,* 61.
5. Ibid., 47, 52.
6. Ibid., 141.
7. Ibid., 59.
8. Berben-Masi, "Prodigal and Prodigy," 677.
9. Guzzio, *All Stories are True,* 184.
10. TuSmith, *Conversations with John Edgar Wideman,* 143.

Chapter 5: Enter Philadelphia

1. TuSmith, *Conversations with John Edgar Wideman,* 106.
2. Ibid., 120.
3. See TuSmith, *Conversations with John Edgar Wideman,* 117.

4. Guzzio, *All Stories are True,* 138.
5. Perrin, "John Edgar Wideman's Urban Inferno," 14.
6. Eschborn, "To Democratize the Elements of the Historical Record," 992.
7. Guzzio, *All Stories Are True,* 29.
8. TuSmith, *Conversations with John Edgar Wideman,* 109, 126.
9. Mbalia, *John Edgar Wideman,* 35.
10. Pearsall, "'Narratives of Self' and the Abdication of Authority," 15.
11. Kendrick, "A Voodoo Guide to the Marginal," 8.
12. Byerman, *The Life and Work of John Edgar Wideman*, 57.
13. Lynch, "The Fever Next Time," 777.
14. Wideman has said that the character is modeled after Richard Allen, the founder of the A.M.E. Zion church, although Allen himself appears in the novel. See TuSmith, *Conversations with John Edgar Wideman,* 185.

Chapter 6: Creolizing Genres

1. Byerman, *The Life and Work of John Edgar Wideman,* 129.
2. Blythe, "Benching Himself," 16.
3. Graham, "Hoop Roots Shows Basketball as a Way of Life, and a Way Out," D2.
4. Jahn, "Will the Circle Be Unbroken?," 58.
5. Guzzio, *All Stories are True,* 35.
6. Bergevin, "Traveling Here Below," 78.
7. Guzzio, *All Stories are True,* 33.
8. TuSmith, *Conversations with John Edgar Wideman,* 94.

Chapter 7: Wideman's Short Fiction

1. There are nine essays under the heading "Fiction" in TuSmith and Byerman's recent collection, but none of them analyzes the short fiction.
2. Champion, "True Stories Are Lies," 77.
3. Byerman, *A Study of the Short Fiction*, 42.
4. Ibid., 35.
5. TuSmith, *Conversations with John Edgar Wideman,* 123.
6. Kellogg, "John Edgar Wideman Takes a Hand in Publishing" (web).

BIBLIOGRAPHY

Fiction and Nonfiction by John Edgar Wideman

Hurry Home. New York: Harcourt, 1970.

The Lynchers. New York: Harcourt, 1973.

Brothers and Keepers. New York: Henry Holt, 1984.

A Glance Away. New York: Holt, Rinehart and Winston, 1985.

The Homewood Trilogy. New York: Avon, 1985.

Reuben. New York: Viking Penguin, 1987.

Fever. New York: Penguin, 1989.

Philadelphia Fire. New York: Henry Holt, 1990.

All Stories Are True. New York: Vintage, 1992.

Fatheralong: A Meditation on Fathers and Sons, Race and Society. New York: Pantheon, 1994.

"Doing Time, Marking Race." *Nation*, October 30, 1995, 503–5.

Introduction to *Live from Death Row*, by Mumia Abu-Jamal. New York: Bard, 1995.

Introduction to *The Best American Short Stories of 1996*, edited by Wideman. Boston: Houghton Mifflin, 1996.

The Cattle Killing. Boston: Houghton Mifflin, 1996.

Damballah. Boston, New York: Mariner, 1998.

Hiding Place. Boston, New York: Mariner, 1998.

Sent for You Yesterday. Boston, New York: Mariner, 1998.

Two Cities. Boston: Houghton Mifflin, 1998.

Hoop Roots: Basketball, Race, and Love. Boston: Houghton Mifflin, 2001.

The Island: Martinique. Washington, D.C.: National Geographic Directions, 2003.

God's Gym. Boston: Houghton Mifflin, 2005.

Fanon. Boston: Houghton Mifflin, 2008.

Briefs. Raleigh, N.C.: Lulu Press, 2010.

Writing to Save a Life: The Louis Till File. New York: Scribner, 2016.

Secondary Works

BOOKS AND CRITICAL ESSAYS

Abu-Jamal, Mumia. "The Fictive Realism of John Edgar Wideman." *Black Scholar* 28.1 (1998): 75–79.

Berben-Masi, Jacqueline. "Prodigal and Prodigy: Fathers and Sons in Wideman's Work." *Callaloo* 22.3 (1999): 677–84.

Bergevin, Gerald. "'Traveling Here Below': John Edgar Wideman's *The Island: Martinique* and the Strategy of Melancholy." In TuSmith and Byerman, *Critical Essays on John Edgar Wideman,* 71–89.

Byerman, Keith. *John Edgar Wideman: A Study of the Short Fiction.* New York: Twayne, 1998.

———. *The Life and Work of John Edgar Wideman.* Santa Barbara, Calif.: Praeger, 2013.

Carden, Mary Paniccia. "'If the City Is a Man': Founders and Fathers, Cities and Sons in John Edgar Wideman's *Philadelphia Fire.*" *Contemporary Literature* 44.3 (2003): 472–500.

Chametsky, Jules. *Black Writers Redefine the Struggle: A Tribute to James Baldwin.* Amherst: University of Massachusetts Press, 1989.

Champion, Laurie. "True Stories are Lies: Postmodern Signifying in John Edgar Wideman's Short Fiction." *Short Story* 19.2 (2011): 60–80.

Coleman, James W. *Blackness and Modernism: The Literary Career of John Edgar Wideman.* Jackson: University Press of Mississippi, 1989.

Danielewicz, Jane. "Double-Voiced Autobiographies." *Life Writing* 9.3 (2012): 269–78.

Eschborn, Ulrich. "To Democratize the Elements of the Historical Record:' An Interview with John Edgar Wideman about History in His Work." *Callaloo* 33.4 (2010): 982–98.

Feith, Michael. "Tourism and Its Discontents: John Edgar Wideman in Martinique." *Revue LISA* 7.2 (2009): 41–58.

Guzzio, Tracie Church. *All Stories Are True: History, Myth, and Trauma in the Works of John Edgar Wideman.* Jackson: University Press of Mississippi, 2011.

Harris, Trudier. *Exorcising Blackness: Historical and Literary Lynching and Burning Rituals.* Bloomington: Indiana University Press, 1984.

Jahn, Karen F. "Will the Circle Be Unbroken? Jazzing Story in *Hoop Roots.*" In TuSmith and Byerman, *Critical Essays on John Edgar Wideman,* 57–69.

Lynch, Lisa. "The Fever Next Time: The Race of Disease and the Disease of Racism in John Edgar Wideman." *American Literary History* 14:4 (2012): 776–804.

Mbalia, Doreatha. *John Edgar Wideman: Reclaiming the African Personality.* Selinsgrove, Penn.: Susquehanna University Press, 1995.

Pearsall, Susan M. "'Narratives of Self' and the Abdication of Authority in Wideman's *Philadelphia Fire.*" *MELUS* 26.2 (2001): 15–46.

Reed, Ishmael. *Airing Dirty Laundry.* Reading, Mass.: Addision, 1993.

Sundquist, Eric. "Fly Away Home: John Edgar Wideman's *Fatheralong.*" *Triquarterly* 126 (2006): 9–28.

TuSmith, Bonnie, ed. *Conversations with John Edgar Wideman.* Jackson: University Press of Mississippi, 1998.

TuSmith, Bonnie, and Keith Eldon Byerman, eds. *Critical Essays on John Edgar Wideman.* Knoxville: University of Tennessee Press, 2006.

BOOK REVIEWS AND JOURNALISM

Blythe, Will. "Benching Himself." Review of *Hoop Roots. New York Times Book Review,* November 4, 2001, 16.

Broyard, Anatole. "A Lynching in Black Face." Review of *The Lynchers. New York Times,* May 15, 1973, 37.

Cheuse, Alan. "Homecoming in Homewood." Review of *Sent for You Yesterday. New York Times Book Review,* May 15, 1983, 12.

Graham, Renee. "*Hoop Roots* Shows Basketball as a Way of Life, and a Way Out." Review of *Hoop Roots. Boston Globe,* October 8, 2001, D2.

Kellogg, Carolyn. "John Edgar Wideman Takes a Hand in Publishing." *Los Angeles Times,* March 29, 2010, accessed November 3, 2015, http://articles.latimes.com/2010/mar/29/entertainment/la-et-john-edgar-wideman29–2010mar29.

Kendrick, Walter. "A Voodoo Guide to the Marginal." Review of *Reuben. New York Times Book Review,* November 8, 1987, 8.

Leonard, John. "There Is No Africa." Review of *Hurry Home. New York Times,* April 2, 1970, 27.

Perrin, Noel. "John Edgar Wideman's Urban Inferno." Review of *Reuben. Washington Post,* November 15, 1987, 14.

Reed, Ishmael. "Of One Blood, Two Men" Review of *Brothers and Keepers. New York Times Book Review,* November 4, 1984, 1, 32–33.

Roskolenko, Harry. "Junkie's Home" Review of *A Glance Away. New York Times Book Review,* September 10, 1967, 56.

INDEX